KETO MEAL PREP

THE ESSENTIAL COMPLETE GUIDE FOR BEGINNERS (EASY, HEALTHY AND WHOLESOME KETOGENIC MEALS RECIPES)

SARAH CAREY

Illustrated by
FORMATNOW

DISCLAIMER

Any application of the techniques, ideas, and suggestions in this document is at the reader's sole

discretion and risk. The author of this document makes no warranty of any kind in regard to the

content of this document, including, but not limited to, any implied warranties of merchantability

or fitness for any particular purpose. The author of this document is not liable or responsible to

any person or entity for any errors contained in this document, or for any special, incidental, or

consequential damage caused or alleged to be caused directly or indirectly by the information

contained within.

CONTENTS

INTRODUCTION   1

CHAPTER ONE: UNDERSTANDING KETOGENIC   3
DIET

CHAPTER TWO: THE MACRONUTRIENT AND   6
MICRONUTRIENT COMPOSITION OF
KETO DIET

CHAPTER THREE: FOODS YOU MUST HAVE IN   22
THE KITCHEN

CHAPTER FOUR: WHAT TO EAT AND WHAT   36
YOU SHOULD AVOID IN A KETO DIET

CHAPTER FIVE: ESSENTIAL KITCHEN GADGETS   42

CHAPTER SIX: KETO-MEAL PLANNING   46

CHAPTER SEVEN: TIPS FOR YOUR SHOPPING   50

CHAPTER EIGHT: EASY KETOGENIC   55
BREAKFAST RECIPES

CHAPTER NINE: SNACKS   85

CHAPTER TEN: DINNER   103

CHAPTER ELEVEN: MAINS   119

CHAPTER TWELVE: DESSERTS, SIDES, SALADS,   129
AND SOUPS

CHAPTER THIRTEEN: SMOOTHIES   171

CONCLUSION   185

INTRODUCTION

Embarking on a nutritional course of ketogenic diet as a quick way of shedding excess weight is one of the fastest growing trends in the world of health and fitness, and it is truly gaining popularity among fitness experts and health-conscious folks alike, especially for those who are likely to get really worried about their ever-increasing waistline!

The effectiveness of utilizing a ketogenic diet to burn fat has never been in doubt, especially when bolstered by scientific studies carried out over the years. However, one key factor that has often hindered enthusiasts, in particular, greenhorns, from getting on this significant life-changing undertaking is the lack of a comprehensive guide and information on how to make a start. Moreover, a lot of people maintain a busy lifestyle that makes it hard for them to adhere to this unique form of diet. For such people, finding the time to do their grocery shopping and to prepare meals can be quite challenging.

This book is an all-encompassing treaty that profoundly walks readers through easy, healthy and wholesome ketogenic meals recipes, and is filled with essential tips and guides that will help them kick start their voyage into the world of this distinctive form of diet that has been proven to be vital and helpful for healthy living.

CHAPTER ONE: UNDERSTANDING KETOGENIC DIET

Keto — A brief history

Fasting is the forerunner to what is known today as the ketogenic diet, and eons ago, it was utilized by men as a means to cleanse the body both physically and spiritually. In retrospect, a lot of the benefits gotten from fasting could be attributable to the presence of ketones in the body. Apparent references to the therapeutic use of fasting in treating ailments like convulsion were made by sages of the ancient world (Hippocrates) and in certain religious texts such as the Bible.

But, until the 20th Century, its proponents never envisaged the critical anticonvulsant effect of ketosis during fasting. It is noteworthy that doctors first noticed a relationship existed between eating a low-carbohydrate diet and fasting in the early part of the 1900s. They also found out that when there is a significant reduction in nutritional intake of carbs and upping the consumption of fat at the same time may reduce the rate of seizures just as in fasting.

However, it was until the 1990s that scientists discovered that fasting might bring about the presence of ketones in the body. Aside from using fasting as a therapy for epilepsy, all through history, high-fat and low-carb diets were employed as a way of treating conditions like diabetes and obesity. In fact, the former had a history of being managed by restricting carb intake.

Although it was first used in the 1920s as a remedy for epilepsy, the ketogenic diet is not an entirely new concept, and the diet has proven to be very effective in the treatment of some variants of epilepsy in children. Similarly, it was found to primarily work well for medical conditions like Lennox-Gastaut syndrome, myoclonic-astatic epilepsy among several others.

'Keto' is derived from the word 'ketogenic,' and refers to a process whereby the body is creating 'ketones' (fuel molecules) from fat. Ketones are an energy source that is essentially different from those obtained from carbs (where the energy derived is usually in the form of glucose) and fats that generally gives the human cells its energy. The keto diet typically consists of meals having a high-fat, moderate amount of protein, and low-carbs.

On consumption for a long period, the keto diet will bring about a metabolic adaptation in the body — thus, giving rise to a state of *ketosis* — and causing the liver to produce ketones from fat, even as the fewer carbs are broken down into blood sugar. The ketones generated from this process then become a source of fuel for the whole body — in particular, the brain which cannot use energy from fat directly but operate on glucose and ketones. It is worthy to note that the brain needs a lot of energy to carry out its daily functions.

When the body is in the state of ketosis, it burns fat for fuel and uses it as a source of energy, and this process could be of tremendous benefit to you if you are trying to improve your performance, shed excess weight or if you want to look slim, trim and fit. Bear in mind that ketosis is able to bring about such changes in weight by keeping the body in a starvation metabolism and then tapping into the body's fat reserves for energy.

However, for ketosis to occur, glucose, the most favored energy source for the body must be evidently lacking. And ketosis can only take place either by fasting or going on a ketogenic diet. The former entails staying away from food so that when the body completely exhausts its glucose store, it is then compelled to begin converting fat to ketones for fuel. On the other hand, the latter method involves taking foods rich in fat that can provide the body with much-needed fuel while avoiding foods that can be easily converted to sugar at the same time.

Quick Tip

The body is said to have attained the state of ketosis when blood ketone levels go beyond 0.5mM.

On average, the time required to reach ketosis after going on a diet of low-carbohydrate and high-fat differs from one individual to another (in some cases, it could take up to a few days or even weeks for the body to produce ketones). However, most people are able to go into a ketogenic state after some days of severe limitations in carb intake. Healthy people that can limit their carb intake but still sustain a sufficient overall intake of calorie will go into this state when the body uses up its glycogen stores. There is a broad range of over-the-counter Ketone Test Strips and Kits that you can utilize to assess the level of ketones in your urine or blood — which gives a direct indication of ketosis.

A BULGING WAISTLINE!

CHAPTER TWO: THE MACRONUTRIENT AND MICRONUTRIENT COMPOSITION OF KETO DIET

As a beginner, once you make up your mind to embrace the changes in lifestyle that often accompany the switch to ketogenic diet — which means cutting down on your fat intake, and making considerable improvement to your health — then it becomes imperative that you alter your body from burning sugar to become the ultimate burner of fat when producing fuel for the body. The question you'd like to ask is how to achieve this?

Well, it is about making changes to what you eat, and it will require you to reduce your consumption of carbohydrates considerably while upping your fat and protein intake. Usually, nearly all keto diets have carbohydrates, protein, and fat, in the proportion of 5%, 20%, and 75% respectively. Indeed, the fats, proteins, and carbohydrate food groups (also called the *macros*) are the three key things that you always need to observe when you are on a keto diet. Since the macros are considered to be the building block of the ketogenic diet, it is pertinent that you understand how they work in order to be successful with the keto diet.

Proteins

Proteins consist of large molecules of chains of amino acids, and play an essential role in keto meal plans because they are vital for growth, and they help increase the body metabolism by building and maintaining lean muscle tissue. In addition, they assist in the regulation of enzymes and hormones, contribute to the structure of red blood cells, and are important for the proper operation of antibodies which, in turn, aids in combating infection. In truth, proteins not only help you become lean but assist you in maintaining a slim and trim figure as well.

Although women don't seem to get sufficient amount of proteins; however, its contribution to keeping the body satiated, assisting with lean mass, and maintain muscle mass and supporting bone density as they grow old cannot be underestimated. Besides, protein is essential for the production of healthy hair, skin, and nails.

SALMON IS A RICH SOURCE OF PROTEIN

As stated earlier, proteins are made of amino acids and are present in a broad range of whole foods. Expectedly, the amino acid content found in foods differs from each other with some having loads of it, while others lack amino acids. Foods like meat, poultry, fish, dairy, and eggs are entirely proteins and contain vital amino acids. Conversely, foods like nuts, nut butter, whole grains, legumes, beans, and some veggies are incomplete proteins — they lack vital amino acids. Some benefits of proteins include:

• The repair and growth of tissues, and preservation of lean muscle tissue

• Playing a critical role in the production of important hormones and enzymes in addition to the immune function

• Having a key role in the way the structural and functional components of cells are set up

• Assist in the secretion of the hormone glucagon — needed to manage insulin and keep its levels under control.

• Allowing for conversion to glucose through the process of gluconeogenesis

• Acting as a source of energy when there is no carb/glucose present

• Supporting the growth of healthy skin, hair, and nails — if you intend to improve your looks, then proteins are essential

• Plays a vital role in metabolic pathways like the Krebs Cycle

Quick Tip

Although protein has the potential of being used as fuel, that is not its main function.

Should you decide to abide by a keto diet, then there is a balance of adequate protein that you need for the sustenance of muscle mass. However, if nutritional protein goes beyond 20-25% of calories, then gluconeogenesis from protein may hinder the creation of ketones. At first, you should aim for a protein consumption of 0.8-1.2g per kg of your body weight as it evens out your protein requirement against the likelihood of too much gluconeogenesis occurring.

It is crucial to bear in mind that the protein needs of certain people (athletes comes to mind) may be high — often requiring an adapted keto macronutrient of fat to non-fat ratio of 2:1 — whereby the standard fat, protein, and carb ratio is at 65%, 30% and 5% in that order, and may still be effective for therapeutic ketosis.

Fats

Basically, fat is made up of triglyceride molecules, and there is a distinction between fat in cells and the diverse types of fat molecules. For instance, *adipose tissue* stores energy as fats/lipid in fat cells (which are also referred to as *Adipocytes*). *Lipids* are a universal term for insoluble and polar biological fat molecules. Its class of molecules includes mono-, di- and triglycerols, cholesterols, and phospholipids. *Triglycerides* are primarily a lipid molecule that has glycerol acting as its basis and is linked to three fatty acid molecules. *Fatty acids* have a molecule containing a chain of carbon atoms linked to each other via carboxylic acid at one end.

Over the years, dietary fat has always been the whipping boy for everything that is wrong in a diet, but on second thought, it seems this bad rap is unjustifiable because fat is a vital source of fuel for the body. When assessed gram for gram, it gives more than double the amount of energy that carbohydrate or protein can give the body. At 9 calories per gram, dietary fat exceeds the 4 given by 1 gram of carb or 1 gram of protein — by more than a factor of 2. When dealing with fat, the crucial thing to take into account is getting the right type of fat and in the right amount as well. Some benefits of fat include:

• Dietary fats enhances energy levels and constitutes major functional and structural aspects of your body system

• It satisfies hunger and longings by making you feel very full for a long period

• Fats assist in raising your HDL cholesterol, which is good cholesterol

• When compared to taking low-fat foods, consuming healthy fats will give you a profound sense of satiety that may assist in controlling your effort to lose weight and stay fit — bear in mind that the chance of eating too much is limited when your body gets a sign that it is not hungry but full and satisfied.

Based on the above reasons, it is imperative to have healthy fats and protein in your keto diet because they do give you a sense of being full and satisfied. Contrary to widely held beliefs, fat is not the foe since it has been proven that its role is significant, in particular, if your objective is shed excess weight and staying lean and fit. However, if you consider the alternative to not eating enough fat, then the implication can be dire for your health because choosing a low-fat, high-carb diet will make you feel hungrier, which, in turn, causes you to consume more food — resulting in more gain in weight.

Quick Tip

In contrast to what you've been made to believe, eating good fat will not make you fat, and it has not been linked with cardiovascular disease!

The question you would like to ask is what type of fats should be included in your keto diet?

• Prior to being stored in the adipose tissue or utilized as fuel, dietary lipids first have to be digested and transported in the bloodstream as triglycerides and fatty acids. And before it is stored in adipose tissue, it must go through strictly regulated metabolic stages. It is essential to bear in mind that dietary fat is not the same as stored fat in the body.

• In a keto diet, Triglycerides occupy a key position because they are responsible for more than 70% of dietary calories. Adherents of the keto diet need to familiarize themselves with how Triglycerides in meals are processed in their body.

• Another source of lipids in diets is fatty acids which could be saturated or unsaturated. The former doesn't have double bonds between carbons while the latter has one or more double bonds between carbons.

• Saturated fats are somewhat stable and have a tendency to be solid at room temperature. Examples of saturated fats include coconut oil, butter, lard, etc.

• There are two types of unsaturated fatty acids — monounsaturated and polyunsaturated fats. The former has one double bond between carbons while the latter is made of multiple double bonds between carbons.

As with fat generally, the consumption of dietary saturated fats have always been restricted over the years, owing to the slander and bad reputation fat had suffered. So, it is not surprising that it has been associated with medical conditions like cardiovascular disease and high blood pressure. But results from recent studies have shown that fat provides the body with plenty of benefits among which includes raising 'healthy' HDL levels.

Quick Tip

The way the fatty acid behaves in and out of the body is a function the number of double bonds it possesses and is a crucial factor to take into consideration.

While unsaturated fats (e.g., olive oil) exist mainly as a liquid at room temperature, they are also regarded as being healthier than saturated fats. In fact, increasing the intake of both types of unsaturated fats have been connected with enhanced blood biomarkers — lower blood triglycerides. When you embark on the keto diet, taking a sufficient amount of unsaturated fats is imperative.

OIVE OIL IS A HEALTHY FAT

The artificial process of adding hydrogen to unsaturated fatty acids so as to solidify and extend its shelf life gives rise to *Trans-fats*. Based on the adverse effect they have on health, the consumption of these types of fat should be done in moderation.

Another excellent fat addition to your ketogenic diet is essential fatty acids such as poly-unsaturated omega-3, omega-6, and omega-9 fatty acids, which the body can't produce naturally. The anti-inflammatory properties of essential fatty acids contribute significantly to health and performance. Essential fatty acids can be derived from foods like sardines, mackerel, hemp seeds, etc.

Another factor that affects the metabolism of fat is the number of carbons in the fatty acid chain. Although the fatty acids chains are able to reach 28 carbons atoms, those that exceed 13 are regarded as long, while those lying between 8-12 are known as medium and fatty acid; carbons atoms less than 5 are called short-chain fatty acid.

Expectedly, the metabolism and absorption of each type of fats differ, with the long-chain fatty acids released straight into the blood after going into the lymphatic drainage system, while the medium and short-chain fatty acids don't have to pass through the lymphatic system. In the case of the latter, they just go straight to the liver having traveled in the blood from the gut. In fact, if a huge amount the short and medium-chain fats gets to the liver at the same time, the liver may set off the process of converting them to ketones, even when there is no constraint on dietary carb intake. Medium-chain fatty acids can be found in either artificially purified or natural forms (coconut oil), and are extremely ketogenic. The use of medium-chain fatty acids is often restricted to increasing ketones artificially since it causes an adverse reaction (e.g., stomach upset) in some individuals.

Quick Tips

• If you plan to incorporate these ideas into your keto diet, then you should target the bulk of the nutritional calories as fat.

• Try and vary the source of your fats by tapping into diverse animal and plant sources like red meat, poultry, fish, dairy, olive oil, coconut oil, nuts, and avocados, etc.

Studies have shown that both saturated fats such as butter and coconut oil and unsaturated fats like olive oil are an essential part of a healthy diet and should play a key role in keto meal plan too. Also recommended is a good amount of heart-healthy omega-3 fatty acid–rich fish in your diet. And if you are a vegetarian, you can acquire the needed amount of omega-3s from flax, hemp and chia seeds.

Although most fats have a similar amount of calories, it is not advisable to include some fats in your diet because they are usually processed and heavily refined as well. Such fats include canola, corn, and soybean oil — also known as vegetable oil. A simple rule to test for the oil to use in your ketogenic diet is to make sure that it tastes like the food from which it is derived. So, what that means, in essence, is that coconut oil must have the taste of coconut! However, the process of making some oils like canola oil tends to strip them of their flavor and aroma because it utilizes chemical and high temperature which denatures fatty acids. Being processed oils, they encourage the formation of free radicals, thereby making them likely carcinogenic, and preventing them from being added to a healthy diet.

As stated earlier, trans fats do not have a good reputation as being healthy because they have been linked to heart diseases and are known to raise LDL levels in the cardiovascular system while lowering HDL levels too. You can find trans fats occurring naturally in foods like meat, butter, and milk, and do not pose any risk to health; however, most trans fats are derived from foods having partially hydrogenated oil. The use of these oils is not encouraged and has been banned from being used in restaurant foods while the U.S. Food and Drug Administration has strict regulations guiding its usage.

Warning!

These unhealthy cheap refined vegetable have a way of making it into your diet; thus you must be vigilant and exercise caution so that they do not.

While we keep emphasizing that fat is neither the problem nor an enemy, the fear of it still lingers in society. In fact, reducing fat in a diet have been shown to be counterproductive because it is likely to make you feel less energetic, more sluggish, and hungrier — which could lead you to binge on foods that don't make you feel full and satisfied. In fact, banishing fat from meals mainly accounts for why the United States is having a lot of fat people. Since eating healthy fat won't cause you to grow fat, so, what are those things/habits that could make you fat?

• An evident lack of exercise

• Taking more calories than you need and can use

• Consuming foods with no nutritional value and calories

• Taking excess refined carbs and sugars

• When your diet lacks the right balance of fats, carbohydrates, and proteins

• When you live a sedentary lifestyle

Carbohydrates

While some people are inclined to argue that carbohydrates are not that important because their dietary protein and fat can serve functions, carbs are a major source of energy and are made of carbon, hydrogen, and oxygen. They are usually found in the form of monosaccharides, disaccharides, and oligosaccharides, with each having single molecule, two-joined molecules, and chains of molecules respectively.

Often called "bad carbs," simple carbohydrates are processed and have little or no nutritional value. Examples of simple carbs include white bread, sugary cereals, sugar and other extremely processed foods that are packaged in boxes or wrappers. The problem with simple carbohydrates is that the body digests them rapidly and effortlessly, thus causing a spike in blood glucose levels which is then followed by quick drops. Consequently, the fluctuation in blood glucose sets off related insulin spikes and drop-offs. The instability (sharp rise and fall) of insulin could adversely impact your attempt to shed excess weight via ketogenic diet; thus it is imperative you try and make the insulin levels stable — simply avoid huge spikes and massive crashes.

Otherwise referred to as "good carbs," complex carbs are loaded with fiber, and the body tends to digests them little by little. Foods found under complex carbohydrates include legumes, beans, seeds, several fruits, and starchy vegetables. The gradual digestion of these carbs makes both the blood glucose and insulin levels stable, thus providing the body with a lot of steady energy to burn and sustain life all through the way.

When put in perspective, complex carbs provide the body a sense of satiety and gives it energy that burns slowly. On the other hand, simple carbohydrates can be digested with ease and converted into sugar in the body — thus causing significant harm to your effort to shed excess weight. When choosing carbs for your keto diet, you should opt for those rich in fiber which comes mainly from vegetables and fruits.

When you are on a keto diet, your consumption of carbohydrates should be extremely low, and this concept differs sharply from most modern western diet which derives its dietary calories from carbs. Taking carbohydrates leads to the release of insulin, which, in turn, prevents the creation of ketones in the liver and stops ketosis as a result. Therefore, it is imperative that you monitor and modulate your carb intake when you are on a ketogenic diet. Dietary carbohydrates perform the following function:

• It replenishes the stores in muscle and liver (glycogen)

• It sustains the concentration of blood glucose so as to give fuel to the entire body, especially for the brain

Assessing blood glucose can be done with ease using a handheld blood glucose monitor. Since the average blood glucose levels rise and fall all through the day and vary from one person to another, it is essential to track it over a long period, especially in reaction to different scenarios like a meal or exercise

POTATOES ARE A SOURCE OF CARBOHYDRATE

Adhering to a keto diet means you must look out for certain concepts like the total amount of carbs, the 'net' amount of carbs (taking related fiber into account), and the rate at which carbs elevate blood glucose — the glycemic index. In a typical ketogenic diet, it is advisable to keep the overall amount of carbohydrates restricted to not more than 5% of energy intake.

Nutritional fiber is carb-based material from plants which is not completely broken down by the small intestine but is rather transported to the large intestine where they are excreted or go through the process of fermentation — that supports the development of useful bacteria. The importance of fiber to a well-planned keto meal plan cannot be overemphasized and includes:

• Maintaining gut health

• It gives the body a feeling of satiety and fullness

Quick Tip!

You should consider adding green and cruciferous veggies to your meals when making plans for your ketogenic diet because they are loaded with fiber.

Based on the nature and source of fiber, the caloric value can be assessed in two different ways. The first method is to assume that fiber has an equal amount of calories per gram as carbohydrates — that is 4 kCal/gram. The second approach utilizes a lower value of 2 kCal/g and assumes that a fraction of fiber is not broken down.

Quick Tip!

Because they are not broken down, digestion-resistant fiber doesn't add to calorie intake.

The net carbs mean the mass of overall carbohydrates, minus the total fiber. For two reasons, this might be an excellent metric to assess carb intake since fiber is mainly resistant to digestion and may not raise blood glucose, and the outcome of many research has revealed that a rise in fiber doesn't impact blood ketone levels.

How rapidly food raises blood glucose after their intake is shown by the 'glycemic index' scale which has a range of 1 to 100. Foods on this scale use pure glucose as a reference because it is set to 100 — implying that it increases blood glucose speedily. But other foods tend to have a relatively lower value since they are likely to raise blood glucose gradually. On the glycemic index, some foods like peanut and white potato have values of ∼15, and ∼80 respectively.

Also, you can calculate the rate of carb release and the overall amount of carbohydrates in food by using the "Glycemic load," as given by the expression below:

Glycemic load = (total carbohydrates [g] x glycemic index) / 1000.

Bear in mind that it is possible for foods to have a fairly high glycemic index and still possess a glycemic load that is extremely low in a serving especially when their total carbohydrate amount is low.

Micronutrients

In contrast to macronutrients like proteins, fats, and carbs which are required in large quantities, micronutrients are needed in much smaller amounts that are critical for good health — hence, the name "micronutrients." The implication of not getting micronutrients in the recommended dosage is an increase in the chances of you developing a medical condition. Micronutrients can mainly be classified into vitamins and minerals. The functions of micronutrients are not restricted to the following:

• Micronutrients act as cofactors during metabolism. An enzyme often requires the presence of Cofactors for it to be active. For instance, Zinc is a common cofactor in the human body and assist in modulating hundreds of enzymes needed for essential functions ranging from protein production to immune system function among several others.

• Micronutrients act as coenzymes in metabolism where vitamins actively take part in the complex biochemical reactions. Typical examples include some b-vitamins like riboflavin, niacin, and folate — all of which takes part in reactions that assist the body in utilizing the foods consumed to give energy, proteins, and nucleic acids.

• Since they might have a direct effect on human genes, micronutrients can assist with genetic control. A case in point is zinc that aids in the regulation of the creation of receptors for steroid hormones and other critical factors.

• Given that micronutrients have excellent antioxidant properties, it makes them suitable for use as antioxidants. For example, antioxidant vitamins such as vitamin E and A can help do away with toxic compounds that have built up in the body during the process of converting food to fuel.

Vitamins

Vitamins are a minute amount of organic compounds that are crucial for the maintenance of regular physiologic function. It is vital to have them in your meals because human bodies can't seem to produce them rapidly enough to meet your everyday needs. They are further subdivided into fat soluble or water soluble vitamins — based on their ability to dissolve in lipids or water. Vitamins that are fat-soluble include Vitamins A, Vitamin D, Vitamin E, and Vitamin K.

Warning!

Do not consume too many fat-soluble vitamins because fat assist in the absorption of these vitamins and they are then stored in fat globules for a long duration.

Unlike fat-soluble vitamins, the water-soluble ones can be taken in excess without any difficulty to the body since they are easily excreted in the urine. Examples include Vitamin C, Vitamin B6, Vitamin B12, Vitamin

H, Thiamin (Vitamin B1), etc. In a ketogenic diet, it is crucial that you pay attention to your micronutrient intake since:

• Your intake of foods rich in micronutrients like fruits and vegetables will be reduced as soon as you lower your carb consumption

• During the first four weeks of being on a keto diet, there is a great chance that the stability of essential micronutrients like sodium, potassium, magnesium, and calcium will be upset owing to a rise in their excretion. Getting used to the diet is the natural way your body will resolve this problem.

The main cation in extracellular fluid is sodium which contributes to blood volume maintenance, water balance, and cell membrane potential. In addition, it is important for acid-base balance and nerve conduction. Once you begin a keto diet, the level of sodium may become low; thus it becomes imperative that you add extra sodium in the form of salt or bone broth to your meal. As a result, you are able to reduce the likelihood of experiencing the common side effects like cramps, which has been linked with a low sodium level in the body.

The main cation in the intracellular fluid is Potassium, and its key duties relate to the maintenance of cell membrane potential and electrical activities in cells like neurons and cardiomyocytes.

Much similar to the way your body reacts to sodium at the start of your keto diet, you are likely to experience a reduction in the levels of potassium owing to increased excretion. Consequently, at the onset of your ketogenic diet, eating foods loaded with potassium like nuts, dark green vegetables, and avocados will help bridge the shortfall.

Another vital element in the biological systems is magnesium, and it contributes to the nerve, muscle, and immune function. A rise in excretion at the start of a ketogenic diet often leads to a reduction in magnesium levels, so foods rich in magnesium like oily fish, dark green vegetables, and seeds will help make up for the deficiency in magnesium when you start your keto diet.

An important micronutrient for cardiovascular and bone health is calcium because it plays a key part in muscle contraction. While a shortage of this essential element is not common during a keto diet, you can augment its level in the body by eating foods rich in calcium such as fish, cheese, and leafy greens.

VITAMINS

CHAPTER THREE: FOODS YOU MUST HAVE IN THE KITCHEN

As soon as you are ready to start your ketogenic diet, there are many keto staples and essentials that you need to stock up in your kitchen or store. What it implies is that you will have to store up stuff like low-carb groceries, keto snacks, and keto sweeteners. Because going on a keto diet is very hard to start, beginners must take one key thing into account — that is preparation is critical and entails having the right information and resources, the right attitude, and a support system that enhances success. So, the planning of your meals and having the right set of foods in your store are some of the factors that underpin the success of your ketogenic diets.

Quick Tips!

• As much as possible, try and replace high-carb foods in your refrigerator or store

• It is crucial that you know the carbohydrate content of different foods

• Bear in mind that carbohydrates are not only present in bread and pastries but are in a relatively fair amount in fruits and veggies

While your ingredient lists do not have to be lengthy, you should still be able to find many ingenious ways to achieve your nutritional objectives by eating a ketogenic diet. The following list of keto-compliant foods will serve as a guide when setting up your keto store or kitchen. Since ketogenic meals tend to differ in terms of net carbs and total carbs, the foods might not fit into your plans flawlessly, so you'll have to alter them to suit your meal plans and specific taste.

Condiments

There are a number of condiments that will boost your ketogenic diet at your local grocery store, and you can tweak some of them to suit your keto diet objectives.

• **Mustard:** Mustards of different variations have zero grams of carbs. For example, spicy brown mustard will be an excellent addition to your store.

• **Ketchup:** They are made of tomatoes and have high carb content. If you are hooked to this condiment, then ketchup with no-sugar-added will be ideal and should be used frugally.

• **Buffalo sauce:** When purchasing this condiment, make sure that there is no sugar added by reading through the label.

• **Mayonnaise:** Again, ensure that there are no unwanted ingredients like added sugar by reading the label.

• **Salad dressing:** Nearly all full-fat salad dressings except sweetened ones are keto-approved. Avoid light salad dressings because its fat is swapped with sugar and ketogenic diet encourages you to take more fat. You may as well get ranch dressing, balsamic vinaigrette, etc.

Oils

Since ketogenic diet profoundly focuses on how you can get plenty of healthy fats into your meals, there are times when attaining your fat acquisition objectives becomes very hard — so hard that you can't get close to the figure until you've added doses of fat to your daily meal plans For instance, you may enhance your bulletproof coffee with fats from butter or coconut oil — thereby upping your daily fat intake while helping you suppress your longings. All health-conscious individuals need to be aware that not all fats are equal. Some important fats include:

• **MCT oil**: The oil, Medium-chain triglycerides (MCT), is a saturated fatty acid — and a derivative of coconut and palm kernel oils. On consumption, the body burns them rapidly rather than storing them. Another benefit of using MCT oil in your meals is that the body converts them to ketones, which, in turn, aids in your fat-burning abilities. You can bring MCT oil into play in your keto meals in a number of ways — pour some over your salads, use them to make healthy dips or add some to your coffee to boost your fat intake.

• **Coconut oil:** Nearly all of its fat emanates from MCT in the form of lauric acid that is utilized as energy by the body. Lauric acid is much similar to carb in the way the body uses it for energy. Lauric acid is good for the heart by raising the level of HDL cholesterol in the blood, thereby enhancing the proportion of HDL and LDL cholesterol. Another benefit of using coconut oil is apparent from the way it eases inflammation, improves energy and endurance, and enhance digestion and absorption of other nutrients like vitamins and amino acids. Additionally, it has a positive impact on blood sugar and may enhance thyroid function — resulting in improved metabolism. Lastly, coconut oil has antifungal, antibacterial, and antiviral properties, and has proven to prevent wrinkles and age spots. When selecting coconut oil for your ketogenic diet, make sure that the label reads "unrefined" or "virgin" so as to prevent the acquisition of low-quality and poorly-processed oil.

• **Cooking oils:** Typical examples of oils under this category include sunflower seed oil, avocado oil, grape seed oil — a distinct feature is that they all have a high smoke points — making them ideal for sautéing, roasting, and stir-frying. In addition, they have a neutral flavor that makes them suitable for baking.

• **Non-cooking oils:** These oils are not stable when subjected to heat — they break down rapidly and could even burn. However, they find application when making soups, delectable salads, etc. Typical examples include flaxseed, walnut, and pistachio oils.

Ghee/Clarified butter

Ghee is obtained when milk solids are browned prior to removing them from clarified butter. It is a source of cooking fat commonly used in India and vaunts a rich, delicious nutty taste. Ghee is loaded with vitamins A, D, E, and K and not only finds application in the kitchen but plays a key role as facial and hair moisturizer — popular among Indian women.

Quick Tip

> Ghee and clarified butter are excellent alternatives for those individuals who can't tolerate dairy.

• Ghee is so delicious that you can eat it by the spoonful just to get the additional fat.

• Ghee can be used to pan-fry vegetables or meats

• Beginners can kick start their journey into the ketogenic diet by engaging more with ghee

Clarified butter has a higher smoke point than olive oil, thus making it better for cooking at a higher temperature. Garlic Powder or Cloves

Quick Tips

> • A smoking point is the point at which the oil starts to smoke, giving toxic fumes and harmful free radicals

> • You can find jars of ghee in Indian groceries or the grocery aisle of natural food stores.

Olives

Olives are loaded with healthy fats that are good for the heart, and you can get them in either green or black color. Not only are they keto-compliant but they also represent the perfect way to infuse some fats into your meals — whether as an addition to salads or you could simply take them as sacks — the ways you incorporate them in your meals are endless. When you go shopping, you may find snack-size single-serve packs in the grocery aisle which can fit into your bag. Other options include the olive bar with marinated and flavored types that can satisfy your cravings as snacks when needed.

Olives go as far back as early human history, and they are similar to what grapes are to wine — meaning that olive oil is affected by variables that could impact its color, aroma, and flavor. When you are shopping for your olive oil, it is best you go for the Extra virgin olive oil because it is the least processed; moreover, it packs the fruitiest flavor and is the least acidic. But, remember that it is quite pricey as well. While Extra virgin olive oil is good for salad dressings but is not the best high-heat cooking oil you will find around — as the temperature goes from low to moderate, it becomes unstable and loses several of its health benefits. In fact, olive oil can best be utilized by drizzling them over foods after it has been prepared.

Some benefits of olive oil include being a monounsaturated oil with no cholesterol and having natural antioxidants that give it anti-inflammatory properties. Olive oil is best known for being a heart-friendly oil and has always been a traditional staple of the people living around the Mediterranean Sea.

Nut Butter

Nearly all the regular peanut butter comes with added sugar, but a growing awareness about the health implication of sugar is causing keto-genic diet adherents to ignore the sweet stuff and opt for unsweetened peanut butter. You may also get unsweetened almond butter, but if you are the adventurous type, then making your own nut butter will be a great idea — to give it an unusual twist, you may add healthy flavors such as cinnamon, vanilla or stevia. Nut butter is good for making dips, spread on smoothies and they also serve as the base of many keto fat dishes that are designed to give you a healthy dose of fats with fewer carbs.

Keto Sweeteners

The choice of sweeteners is dependent on the keto dieter as some prefer using artificial sweeteners while others are inclined to ignore them. Whether you are trying to make healthy baked goods or pancakes, you have the choice of using keto-approved sweeteners like stevia, monk fruit, sucralose, and erythritol. It is essential to take into account the fact that these keto-approved sweeteners taste sweeter than the artificial ones like the granulated sugar, and may not always work well for baking. So, it pertinent you get keto recipes that that work well for these sweeteners should you decide to opt for them.

Snacks

Snacks filled with carbs are definitely not an option in a ketogenic diet. Luckily, there are many keto-friendly options you can fall back on when hunger pains begin to set in, especially when you have a tight schedule and need to buy some time. It is vital for you to know that snacks shouldn't be an everyday thing, because keto diets are designed to make you stay for a long period without food. However, if you take snacks frequently, then you may have to up the fat intake in your meals.

Easy whole foods: Not only do they have very low carbohydrates, but these savory snacks are also meant to ward off hunger for some time, and the amazing thing about them is that they do not require much time to prepare. Typical examples include olives, fatty cold cuts, and slices of bacon, avocado, a slice of cheese and hard-boiled eggs (goes well with butter or a keto dip). If you are not allergic to nuts, then low-carb options like Brazil nuts, macadamia nuts, and pecan nuts should be appropriate. Furthermore, other excellent choices include pork rinds, cheese crisps, beef jerky (biltong), and meat snacks (meat bars and sticks).

Vegetables and dips: There are a number of low-carb vegetable options that you can avail yourself of when hunger sets in. Examples of such veggies include cucumber, celery, pepper (red, green, and yellow), and carrot (tends to be quite high on carbs). These vegetables do quite well with cream cheese, sour cream, and low-carb dip sauce.

Berries: Whether fresh or frozen, having berries occasionally is great when you are on a keto diet, but taking them in excess could be counter-productive and reverse your ketosis. Berries that best serve this purpose are Strawberries, Raspberries, Blueberries (have more carbs), and Black-berries. You can take things up a notch by dipping your berries into fat-laden whipping cream — letting the natural sweetness to be assertive, without having to add any artificial sweetener. The danger with this tasty snack is that you may get carried away and overeat, and hurt your weight loss effort as a result!

Chocolates: It may be surprising for you to find chocolate on the keto diet, but you will have to exercise a great deal of caution by taking them in little quantity. Additionally, you must stay away from the dark, milk, and white chocolates because of their high carb content.

Pork rinds: These snacks come in a variety of names (e.g., pork crisps and cracklings) and have very low carb too. They will no doubt come in handy when you have to satisfy your longings with crunchy snacks. When doing your shopping, you should consider buying artisanal pork rinds because they taste better than commercially produced pork rinds.

Beef jerky: If you don't want to buy commercial brands with plenty of artificial sweeteners, you may decide to make your own beef jerky. More-over, you should read the labels carefully so as to pick the ones having the least amount of carbs.

BEEF

Biltong: This meat snack contains no added sugar and could be made from dried spiced beef, venison or ostrich. Also, it is possible to make your own Biltong at home.

Herbs And Supplements To Spice Up Your Foods

You can improve your ketosis by utilizing herbs and supplements that adds flavor and nutrient to your meals without having to raise the overall calories of the food significantly. Besides, the combination of these herbs and supplements can help spark off your creativity in the kitchen as well.

Lemon/Lime Juice: Both are of the citrus family and are loaded with citric acid and vitamin C. They assist in preventing wrinkles, and enhancing the immune system; they are anti-oxidants that aids in improving insulin signaling and stabilizing blood sugar. They also play a crucial role in digestion and the detoxification of the body, while improving your mood and energy, and helping the body burn fat for fuel.

Quick Tips

• For detoxification in the morning, simply squeeze lemon or lime in hot water.

• Lemon or lime can also be added to salads, green juices, meat, and cooked vegetables in order to enhance ketosis.

Cinnamon: This anti-oxidant aids in the regulation of blood sugar level, assists in digestion, enhances blood circulation, reliefs' joint pains and muscle stiffness, and relieves menstruation cramps. Cinnamon can be used by applying them to shakes and ketogenic dessert recipe. Besides, when there is a need to cycle out of ketosis by using high carb foods like carrots, sweet potatoes, pumpkin and yams, cinnamon can be utilized to lower their effect on blood sugar level. Additionally, it can be an excellent addition to your coffee or oatmeal.

Garlic: Having garlic available in your store or kitchen is important for the success of your ketogenic diet because it acts as a vital flavoring in many Keto condiments.

Warning!

Avoid taking garlic in excess as it may throw you out of ketosis. The reason being that garlic contains net carb.

Apple Cider Vinegar (ACV): It is rich in acetic acid, and its use in meals has been proven to lower the glycemic response of a normal carb meal significantly. Also, apple cider vinegar has an enzyme that boosts the metabolism of protein and fat. ACV is easy to use, and all that it requires is to apply it to foods and purified water directly.

Fermented Foods: These types of foods come in various forms like coconut milk yogurt, tofu, coconut milk kefir, kombucha, sauerkraut, pickles and kimchi among several others. Fermented foods are of immense benefit to the body because they improve digestion, and are loaded with enzymes and help in the restoration of beneficial bacteria to the gut. In addition, fermented foods have natural acids that stabilize blood sugar levels while the probiotics, enzymes and other bioactive nutrients it contains assists in enhancing digestion and improving ketosis. The best way to take advantage of them is to eat different fermented foods every day while focusing on those that give you satisfaction and satiates your taste buds when eating them.

Quick Tip

It is best you eat fermented foods at the start of the meal itself, as it gives enzyme support and probiotics that assist the body in metabolizing the remaining food that you will eat later.

Turmeric: This gold-colored spice is an integral aspect of Oriental medicine which packs plenty of benefits for the keto dieter. Its active compound *Curcumin* is a potent anti-inflammatory compound that soothes chronic inflammatory mediated disease processes. Also, it helps modulate blood sugar and reduce the activity of certain liver enzymes that release sugar into the bloodstream, even as it activates enzymes that store sugar as glycogen. In addition, curcumin was discovered to stabilize and lower triglyceride levels in type-2 diabetes patients — thereby improving ketosis since your blood sugar levels are stabilized.

You can get the best out of turmeric when it is added to an excellent fat source, and then adding black pepper to assist in activating the curcumin. It can also be a great addition to smoothies, green drinks, and meat and vegetable dishes. In order to optimize Turmeric's anti-oxidant properties, it advisable that you add it to your food after you've finished preparing it.

Fenugreek Seed: These tiny seeds are bitter and have a pungent smell. Since ancient times, they have been used to improve digestion, while studies have shown them to enhance kidney health, directly stimulate insulin, and to lower high serum cholesterol and triglycerides. Fenugreek seed can be administered directly with meals so as to maintain stable blood sugar and to enhance ketosis.

Chilies: There are a variety of chilies that can help bring your taste buds to life. You may select from a list of mild ones that includes like jalapeños, cherry peppers, and Spanish pimientos while habanero, Scotch bonnet, and the ghost chilies are spicier and hot ones to pick from if you are daring enough! Chilies raise endorphin production and metabolism, soothes pain, support heart health, and stop ulcers. When doing your shopping, always read the labels of hot sauce and stay away from those with plenty of sugar and artificial ingredients.

Bitter Gourd: This fruit is native to India and tastes bitter — hence, the name. It is a potent insulin manager and provides the body with excellent blood sugar support — making it a powerful antidiabetic drug (which is already accepted in China). To improve ketosis, bitter gourd can be taken with meals.

Herbs: They are varieties of incredible flavors that you need to make delectable meals. Common herbs include rosemary, oregano, cilantro, and thyme. Although you won't find them in processed foods, you can get them at the local grocery store, and if there is space in your garden, you may decide to grow and have them fresh when needed.

Flours and Thickeners

In a ketogenic diet, the regular all-purpose flour is not well-suited for baked goods and thickeners. Perhaps you love making pancakes, muffins, waffles, and cookies so much that not having them would make you feel like the world is coming to an end! Well, you don't have to fret about that because there are plenty of healthy keto-approved alternatives that you can draw on if the need to bake or make soups and sauces arises.

These substitutes come in the form of low-carb and fiber-rich healthy options like almond flour, almond meal, and coconut flour — they pack excellent nutty flavor as well — therefore, making them ideal for your muffins, waffles, keto cookies, etc. Also, healthy alternatives you can utilize as thickeners for stews and soups as opposed to the all-purpose flour are almond and coconut flours, while xanthum gum and guar gum — both fiber-rich thickeners — are an excellent substitute for the all-purpose flour when there is a need for texture and viscosity in your dish.

Salt

Salt is a vital aspect of a keto diet, and having quality ones around you will be a great boost to weight loss effort because it helps stabilize and relief the body during the process of burning fat for fuel, especially when it is prone to electrolyte swings. During ketosis, the body lacks reserves to hold on to water, thereby causing you to urinate repeatedly. What it means in effect is that you are losing a great deal of sodium and electrolytes than the ordinary person would, thus necessitating the need to swap it with salt. In fact, you will find the process of doing that enjoyable!

During shopping, avoid buying the refined white salt — the common table salt — because it is industrially processed and lacks essential natural minerals which have been removed during processing. Alternatively, the healthy type of salt to stock up is the unrefined salt like sea salt and Himalayan salt — both of which contains a lot of minerals and nutrients that the body needs. The benefits of unrefined salts include:

• Eating unrefined salt helps you lose and maintain weight because it produces digestive juices that assist the body in digesting and assimilating foods rapidly

• It is contributes to the preservation of melatonin and serotonin which elevates your mood and makes you feel relaxed enough to sleep well

• It has a negligible amount of potassium which is essential for the proper functioning of the muscles. While working out, the body tends to lose plenty of sodium when you sweat, and these vital mineral needs to be replenished during exercise.

• Unrefined salts help curb your craving for food because it gives you a feeling of being full and satisfied when added to foods. When used creatively, you can satiate your longings without sacrificing the health benefits of your keto diet.

Quick Tip

Due to processing, refined salt is often comes as white. In contrast, unrefined salts like sea salt are off-white to gray in color. Better still, you could opt for Himalayan salt which is loaded with of minerals and trace elements that the body can metabolize efficiently.

Aside from unrefined salts, there are other types of quality flavored salts you can utilize as a keto dieter. For instance, Herbes de provence salt is good for soft goat cheese while a dash of smoked salts is great on meats.

Low-Carb Veggies

A ketogenic diet requires vegetables with low calories and carbohydrate contents and must also be loaded with nutrients, vitamins, and minerals. The type of vegetables that fits that bill is the non-starchy veggies because unlike other carbohydrates, they lack fibers that the body can't digest and absorb. In general, the net carb count for non-starchy veggies are quite low, and their benefits include:

• Having antioxidants that aids in protection from free radicals (unstable molecules) that could severely harm the body cells

• Besides, cruciferous veggies such as kale, broccoli, and cauliflower could help lower the risks of developing cancer and heart disease risk

• Being able to substitute foods high in carbohydrates with low-carb vegetables. For example, you can create a form of rice and noodles from cauliflower and zucchini respectively.

Quick Tips

• Here, it is vital to watch out for the digestible (or net) carb count — the total carbs minus fiber.

• Avoid buying starchy veggies like potatoes, yams, and beets because they could make you exceed your daily carbohydrate intake.

Examples of great nonstarchy veggies are asparagus, avocados, mustard, spinach, Swiss chard, asparagus, avocados, tomatoes, bok choy, celery, and eggplant. Also, you may consider matcha, romaine, watercress, cucumbers, fennel, green beans, jicama, okra, snap peas, among several others.

Other Essential Foods

Seafood: Clams, salmon, crab, squid, lobster, mussels, sardines, mackerel, octopus, oysters, scallops, and shrimp.

Dairy: Cheese of varying types like cream cheese, goat, gouda, muenster, provolone, Swiss cheese, buffalo mozzarella, and brie. Along with eggs, harder cheese like mozzarella, parmesan, cheddar, feta, and Havarti are recommended. Also, you can add cottage cheese, Greek yogurt, mascarpone, ricotta, and whole milk to your store/pantry.

Other essential things to take into account include hot sauce like mustard and vinegar, and canned foods (fish or seafood). In addition, you should consider getting Bouillon cubes and broth, and beverages like club soda, coffee, and tea. Besides, unsweetened cold brewed coffee or iced tea will be a great addition as well.

CHAPTER FOUR: WHAT TO EAT AND WHAT YOU SHOULD AVOID IN A KETO DIET

For your keto diet to be successful, there are certain foods you should avoid because they not only going to put you out of ketosis but harm your weight loss effort significantly (if that is what you are trying to achieve in the first instance).

Carbohydrates

Grains: You should avoid eating foods in this sub-type of carbohydrates because taking them in excess can mess up ketosis and hinder weight loss ultimately. Such foods include maize, oats, Quinoa, rice, sorghum, millet, wheat, barley, rye, sprouted grain, buckwheat, etc.

Legumes: While these foods are ideal for people on a regular diet, they are not suitable for those on a keto diet because their carb content is high. Foods in this sub-category of carbohydrate include beans of various types like black-eyed peas, lentils, kidney beans, pinto beans, chickpeas, black beans among several others.

Fruits

A widely held belief is that eating fruit is good for the health, and that assertion to an extent is true; however, it does not mean that they are compatible with a ketogenic diet. Regardless of the type and nature of the fruits, whether fruit juices, dried fruits, fruit smoothies or tropical fruits, they are not allowed in allowed in a keto diet. But if there is a need for you to eat fruits, then you should opt for those that are low in sugar content such as blueberries, blackberries, and raspberries, and above all, to take them infrequently. Fruits to avoid are bananas, tangerine, apples, grapes, mangoes, papaya, fruit concentrates, and syrups.

Starchy Vegetables

While you are on a keto diet, it is essential that you lay more emphasis on leafy greens, and to stay away from veggies that are grown underneath the ground. The major issue with these foods is that they have high starch content. Examples include yams, potatoes, parsnips, peas, yucca, corn, and cherry tomatoes.

Sugars And Its Substitutes

Sugar comes with a plethora of names in food labels, and are so concealed that it is hard for you to find them. Aside from throwing you out of keto-sis, other adverse effects of sugar and its substitutes are that:

• Their sweetness causes the body to anticipate more calories which may not be forthcoming, thereby causing it to search somewhere else for it — meaning that it takes more calories to bridge the gap in order to satisfy the longing. The overall effect of eating them will drive you further away from achieving your health and fitness objectives

• In addition, sugar and many artificial sweeteners are so sweet that they can interfere and ruin your taste buds. Frequent consumption of foods and beverages with a significant amount of artificial sweeteners will make your taste buds to become accustomed to their sweetness in due course. The outcome is that your taste buds will not be able to recognize real foods that are sweet (like berries) because it is already used to tasting sweeter things!

Sugars to stay away from while on keto diet are honey, raw sugar, agave nectar, maple syrup, cane sugar, and high fructose corn syrup (HFCS).

Protein

You can take a lot of protein when you are on a keto diet but you should, as much as is possible, avoid eating inferior proteins. The two major types of protein to avoid are:

Milk and low-fat dairy: While dairy products such as yogurt, butter, heavy cream, and sour cream are keto-compliant, you will still have to stay away from other forms of milk and low- and reduced-fat dairy products. They are considered harmful to your keto diet program because not only do they have unsafe hormones, their carbohydrate content is high, and most individuals find it challenging to digest pasteurized milk — mainly due to the lack of beneficial bacteria. You may take raw milk in little quantity — one serving daily should suffice. But make sure that you consider net carbs. The types of dairy products you should avoid include evaporated milk, shredded cheese, low-fat cream cheese, low-fat whipped toppings, fat-free yogurt, milk, and fat-free butter substitute.

Factory farmed animal products: When sourcing for foods for your keto diet, you should opt for organically raised animals which are grass-fed while avoiding grain-fed meats and dairy since they have fewer nutrients. Additionally, fish and pork products with a high amount of omega-6s that are farmed in the factory should be avoided. In fact, fish farmed in that manner have been shown to contain a high amount of mercury. Other related foods to avoid are hot dogs and packaged sausages because they have nitrates that are unsafe and even likely cancerous.

Fat

Although the fat you consume in your keto diet is important, the quality of fat is essential as well. Given that fat will constitute most of your meals; therefore a ketogenic diet based on high-quality fat would naturally give healthier meals. In a keto diet, the only type of fat to avoid completely is vegetable oils.

Inflammatory vegetable oils: Saturated and unsaturated fat are an excellent source of fat and include healthy oils like coconut oil, virgin olive oil, and macadamia nut oils — which are mainly not processed. Harmful oils to avoid are grape seed oil, soya bean oil, safflower oil, sunflower oil, peanut oil, sesame oil, canola oil, and corn oil.

Drinks

It is advisable to carry on drinking water when you are on a keto diet. Do not take sugar-free beverages, and avoid soft drinks and alcohol with high carb content.

Water: You may take water with ice or have it like hot tea; you could even drink it when it is flavored naturally with sliced cucumber, lemon, or lime.

WATER

Coffee: Your coffee should be taken without sugar, but a little quantity of milk or cream should be okay. In order to raise its fat content, you may add butter or coconut oil.

Quick Tip

If your keto dieting goal is to shed excess weight and you observe that you are not dropping enough weight as you ought to, then you may have to reduce the amount of cream or fat in your coffee.

Tea: There are different types of tea, and they include green, black, orange, mint, and herbal. The drinking of tea is allowed in a keto diet, but you must not add sugar.

Bone broth: This is an excellent beverage to add to your keto diet. Not only can you make it at home, but it is also easy to prepare and are loaded with vital nutrients and electrolytes that will leave you feeling refreshed, hydrated, and satisfied. You may even choose to add some butter so as to give it some bite and energy.

High carb alcohol: Aside from having some amount of carbohydrate content which is not good for your keto diet, it could hold up the shedding of excess fat during the process of ketosis too. Alcohol drinks with high carb content include cocktails, beers, wine, flavored syrups, sodas, and flavored alcohol.

Sweetened and sugary beverages: These drinks have plenty of carbs, and it is advisable that you steer clear of them, especially when you are on a ketogenic diet. Typical examples include all diet sodas, most diet sodas, all sugar-sweetened drinks, fruit and vegetable juices, sweetened milk products, and sweetened coffee and tea drinks.

Processed and packaged foods

Packaged and processed foods are filled with sweeteners, stabilizers, trans fats, preservatives and other chemicals that are harmful to the body. So when you are on a keto diet, you should avoid taking unhealthy processed products like ice creams, candies, commercially baked goods, and wheat gluten, among several others. So, you must focus on whole foods that are unprocessed and packaged.

Warning!

You must exercise caution when you see "low-carb" or "zero-carb" on labels, as it could mean they are low in carb content per serving, which, in turn, may not be satisfying. Also, there is a likelihood that gluten, sweeteners, flavors and artificial additives may have been used during preparation.

Artificial Sweeteners

They can be regarded as one of the worst agents of poor, unhealthy diet and must be avoided at all cost in a keto diet. Not only are they detrimental to health, but they also cause a spike in blood sugar levels. Typical examples include aspartame, saccharin, sucralose, Splenda, and acesulfame.

Condiments

In contrast to buying them from the grocery store, it is advisable that you make condiments at home since it allows you to use healthy ingredients like herbs and spices during preparation. However, if you have to buy them from the grocery store, then you must steer clear of those condiments that are made with unhealthy oils (listed earlier), contains *added sugar,* and have the *low-fat* labels.

CHAPTER FIVE: ESSENTIAL KITCHEN GADGETS

There some essential kitchen gadgets that will make life comfortable for you when you are on a keto diet — especially when they help make difficult and arduous cooking tasks required for delicious meals to look easy. It is possible that some of them are in your kitchen by now, so you may not have to bother buying them any longer.

Food Scale

This gadget is important for taking measurements of servings, and assessing how much of macronutrients you will be eating. When you take measurements during meal preparation, it:

• Considerably minimizes the margin of error for different ingredients

• Let's you see flaws in the recipes

• Helps make your recipes taste better

An electric scale is designed to make you accomplish a lot while in the kitchen, and it also lets you change from grams to ounces or vice versa.

A FOOD MEASURING SCALE

Measuring Cups And Spoons

Since you don't need a food scale to measure everything in the kitchen, measuring cups and spoons can handle such tasks easily.

Slow Cooker

The slow cooker gives you the freedom to engage in other things while it cooks whatever is placed inside it slowly — this is usually reliant on the settings.

Slow Cooker Liners

These are innovative, not reusable liners that can be cleaned with ease after use, thus saving you a great deal of time.

Frying Pan

A frying pan is another essential kitchen gadget. For example, it may come in handy when you want to fry some vegetables in fat. When looking for a frying pan, one with a heavy base which spreads the heat evenly and makes it constant is something you should consider.

Spiralizer (Benchtop, Handheld)

You won't be able to pull off low-carb without one successfully. This is a fun tool to use in the kitchen, and there is no way you can go on a low-carb diet without it. They are primarily used to make perfect and better substitutes for pasta. With either of these tools, you can make varying sizes of healthy zoodles or ribbons of "pasta. However, you must exercise a great deal of caution when working with the handheld type, as its exposed blades could result in cuts to the fingers. Conversely, the bench top type is fast, safe-to-use, and can be washed with ease.

An Ingredient Cookbook

An ingredient cookbook that will serve as a guide to help you make quick, delicious and easy meals in the kitchen.

Cutting Boards

A cutting board is a platform for you to do all your chopping. On the cutting board, various items like vegetables, meat, fish, etc., can be chopped to sizes that suits your need. Not only is it portable, but it is easy to use, clean and handle as well.

Food Processor

This is an essential tool that a kitchen cannot do without. Whether you want to shred, mix, chop or puree vegetables, flour, or any ingredient for that matter, then this tool comes in handy to help achieve your culinary objectives. So if you want to continue making healthy smoothies and soups, then it is best you acquire this indispensable gadget that saves you a lot of time too.

Mixing Bowls

Regardless of the type of mixing bowls you can acquire, they help save space when used as storage in the refrigerator or kitchen cabinet. Some mixing bowls are stackable while others come with lids.

Baking Trays and Cake Tins

You will be doing the occasional baking of healthy cakes and pastries when you go on a keto diet, and that is exactly where baking trays and cake tins come into play.

Cast Iron Kit

This gadget is the ideal skillet for the boiling of meat or veggies and can be used in the oven and on the cooker too.

Roasting Pan

As the name implies, a roasting pan is a gadget that helps you cook meat, veggies and other types of food in the oven, especially when you have to do that on a frequent basis.

Knives, Mortars, And Pestles

Excellent, solid knives of varying sizes are a must-have for any modern kitchen because they are safe and easy to use, and make your cooking faster as well. Conversely, mortars and pestles are used for crushing or grinding herbs, granulated sweetener or any other ingredient that you wish to grind/crush.

Coffee And Ice-Cream Makers

While it is something you could do without in the kitchen, but having a coffee-maker available will not only make life easy for you but help whip up refreshing and enjoyable coffee drinks that are also sugar-free and keto compliant!

Just like the coffee maker, an ice-cream maker is an optional gadget you may install in the kitchen, but there is nothing that delights children more than the sight of a healthy fluffy and sugar-free ice cream!

CHAPTER SIX: KETO-MEAL PLANNING

Planning is a crucial factor that will determine the success or failure of your ketogenic diet. As a result, there are simple steps that you must follow in order to create a meal plan that suits your ketogenic diet objectives — in effect, your needs and macro goals.

Set SMART Goals

You need to set goals that are SMART (specific, achievable, realistic, and time-bound). In doing that, you must answer some crucial questions about why you want to go on a keto diet. It is likely that you have put on more weight over the years and would like to shed a lot of it. Perhaps, your waistline is increasingly becoming enlarged, and you want to put a stop to the worrisome trend. In addition, it could be that you want a proven method that enhances your mental alertness and improves your energy level at the same time. Besides, you could use a keto diet to help reduce your blood sugar and cholesterol levels so as to boost your health and fitness considerably.

Regardless of what your objectives are for wanting to go on a keto diet, you must write them down somewhere so that you can see them all the time. A simple way to achieve this is to create a vision board. All you have to do is get the image and picture, phrase, or word that not only appeals to you but stand for your goals and those things you want to accomplish with the keto diet. Get a poster board and use gum, glues, and tapes to paste these things into a collage. Afterward, position the vision board where it can serve as a source of inspiration for you — preferably in the bedroom where it becomes the first thing you see in the morning and the last thing you see at night. When you can put these things in place, sticking to a keto diet will be a lot easier for you.

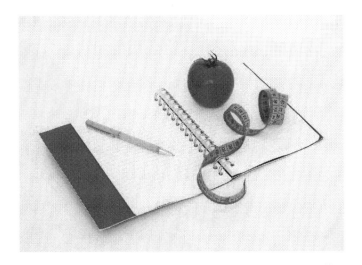

WRITE DOWN YOUR GOALS

PIX CREDIT: WWW.PIXABAY.COM

Measure Your Macros

Calculating the ratios of your macronutrient intake is essential to a keto diet. In general, the macro ratio of your diet would require that 70-80% of your calorie intake should be high fat, while the protein and low-carbohydrate contents are 20-25% and 5-10% or less, respectively. While the calculation of your macros is no rocket science, you can take consolation in the fact that some excellent online resources will be of great assistance regarding this task. For example, there are keto macro calculators that will assist you in finding out the category of what to eat and in what amount to take them, depending on your body composition and lifestyle. Moreover, you will get a fair estimate of the quantity of fat, protein, and carbs that should be in your meals for a day.

Plan Your Meals

Depending on your daily macros, you can take time out to plan your meals for the next one week. As soon as you have made plans for a week, it becomes a template for subsequent meal plans, and you can then tweak it with recipes downloaded from the internet so that you will have something exciting to look forward to each week. Besides, there are intuitive online apps that will help you calculate the macros and calorie count of recipes that don't have this information listed against them. A simple search on the internet will give you lists of the right foods for the ketogenic diet meals. A guide that will assist you with your planning each day is to take the following into account and write them down:

• The number of servings you will be making for each meal, and which is a function of the number of people that will be taking part in them

• What you intend to do with leftovers and whether you should have enough for the following day.

• The daily structure of your meals — whether you want to skip breakfast and take lunch and dinner or not.

As soon as the plan of your meals is complete, you will have to draw up a shopping list with the ingredients for each meal before heading for the grocery store to buy them.

Start Cooking

Once you've planned out your meals, and gotten the right ingredients, it is time to look at the specifics and start cooking the meals. There are many options available to you. You may choose to dedicate a whole day to prepare and cook all the meals you need and then put them away in storage until when the opportunity to use them arises during a busy week. Also, you may decide to cook each meal as already planned out in your keto meal plan.

Quick Tip

When making plans for your cooking you must take into consideration your schedule and lifestyle because making drastic changes can have a devastating effect, but a good plan will help cushion that and lead you to success.

CHAPTER SEVEN: TIPS FOR YOUR SHOPPING

When you go to the local grocery or supermarket to acquire things that you need to get your ketogenic diet going, there are some useful tips, guidelines, and habits that you must imbibe, which will help lessen the stress and pressure of shopping. While there are specific things you will have to do if you want to save time and money and to get fresh organic foods, in general, grocery shopping is an enjoyable activity if you know what you want and how to get them.

Don't shop when you are hungry: The logic behind this guideline lies in the fact that when you go shopping on an empty tummy, there is a tendency for you to make the wrong decisions because the momentary craving you are experiencing will interfere with your judgment and cause you to make impulsive acquisitions. In order to put your longings under control, some low-carb snacks like almonds and plenty of water will help stem the effect of the hunger, and prevent you from making any rash decisions — like stocking up on high-carb foods!

Shop outside the perimeter of the store: You are likely to find real fresh foods at this part of the store, whether you are looking for seafood, seeds and nuts, meats or veggies, you will certainly get them there. Conversely, the inside of most stores is usually filled with processed and packaged foods like cans, boxes, and bags of food. With this information, you can easily stroll into the grocery store to pick your weekly supplies of fresh foods.

Go through the labels: It is important that you read through the labels of the items you want to buy just to ensure that they meet your keto diet requirements. Also, you should return foods that are heavily processed back to the shelf — because you wouldn't want too many chemicals to interfere with your keto diet — in fact, the more natural the foods are, the better they are for you.

Be wary of labels with bold claims: While foods that are not processed do not carry a label, you should exercise caution when dealing with foods that make bold claims about their content. For instance, it is not unusual to find a canned/packaged food with the phrase "no added sugar" or "low-carb" on its label; even though you may be tempted to put it in your shopping cart, it is crucial you do your research by reading the label, and then see if there are better options.

In most cases, such foods, whether pasta, bread, cookies, etc., are often loaded with ingredients like starch, sweeteners, additives, preservatives, etc., that will cause you more harm than good. Also, another thing that could set the alarm bells ringing, and which you must ignore are words like "cereal," "cookie," "bread," "cracker," etc. Moreover, you must disregard highly processed foods with phony labels like "healthy," "natural," and adhere to natural, delicious keto foods.

Warning!

When going through the label of a canned or packaged food, if there are ingredients you find hard to pronounce their names, then it means the food is heavily processed. Please put them back on the shelf!

Make bulk purchases: When you master the art of buying your supplies in bulk, it will not only save you time but a lot of money as well. A key factor to achieving this is knowing stores that sell items in huge amount — e.g., the freezer and produce sections. The internet is another place where you can make bulk purchases. Storing up foods like meat, dairies, veggies, frozen berries, etc., in bulk allows you to quickly put your meals together, thus saving you much needed time.

Steer Clear Of Processed/Packaged Foods: As stated earlier, foods that are significantly processed are not real foods and must be avoided at all cost because they often contain sugar and its substitutes, starch, and fats that could pose a grave danger to your health.

Buy less fruit and high-carb veggies: Since you will be taking them intermittently, avoid stocking too much of keto-compliant fruits and berries, while lemon and lime should be taken in a small amount as well. Also, avoid stocking up on high-carb vegetables.

Buy fewer nuts and less dark chocolate: Although it is advisable to eat nuts and dark chocolate, they should be taken in small quantities because their taste and availability make it likely that you'll eat too much of them, thereby throwing you out ketosis. You will have to consult guides on nuts and snacks to find out the best options that suit your keto diet and to know the carb content of the different types of chocolate.

Warning!

There is also the probability of you eating too many baked foods made from almond flour, so it vital that you watch out for the amount of almond flour you buy at the grocery store and the portion size too.

Avoid Bad Ingredients

Since most processed/packaged foods have a list of ingredients, it is imperative that you go through this list before adding any food to the shopping cart. There are four things to stay away from when you are on a keto diet, and they are sugar, grains, Trans fats and processed vegetable oils.

Sugar: As stated earlier, sugar comes in many forms and manufacturers have mastered the art of masking them in many products — even on food labels! So, you need to be wary of foods having sugar, syrup, malt or cane product as part of its ingredient. Other things to watch out for in regards to sugar include ingredients ending with 'ose' (such as lactose), and stuff like honey, fruit juice concentrates and dried fruit.

Grains: For obvious reasons, you must avoid grains because they add a significant amount of carbs to a diet. The fact that nearly all starch in our meals is from grains goes further to bolster the above point — indeed, wheat and corn are notable culprits here. Grains and their derivatives which comes in the form of all types of flour not only add to the carb content of food products but can put an end to your state of ketosis too!

WHEN YOU GO SHOPPING

Trans fats and processed vegetable oils: Even though adherents of keto are encouraged to focus on fat, fats, themselves, differ from one another. A key shopping tip is to get fats that are natural and to steer clear of altered and industrially extracted fats. You must by all means avoid:

• **Trans fats** — things that are partly hydrogenated or any ingredient like margarine.

• **Processed vegetable seed oils** — obtained from cottonseed, grapeseed, canola, corn, and soybean oils.

Artificial sweeteners and related chemicals: These are known to seriously harm your effort to live a healthy life because they hinder weight loss and cause you to become hooked on sugar. The best way to deal with the addiction to artificial sweeteners and related chemicals is to avoid and banish the craving they bring to your life while doing your shopping.

Sugar alcohols like erythritol and xylitol: Lastly, you should stay away from sweeteners derived from chemicals such as sucralose and aspartame.

CHAPTER EIGHT: EASY KETOGENIC BREAKFAST RECIPES

Having gained sufficient knowledge about what ketosis is all about, the foundation on which the keto diet is built, and what to eat and what you shouldn't eat, then it is time to get to the crux of the matter — making easy healthy and wholesome keto breakfasts.

A KETO BREAKFAST

SPAGHETTI SQUASH PATTIES WITH AVOCADO AND POACHED EGG

Cook Time: 45 mins

Prep Time: 10 mins

Serves: 2

Ingredients:

2 medium spaghetti squash

2 Tbsp. of avocado oil

2 Tsp. of Himalayan salt

1 Avocado

2 pastured eggs

2 Tbsp. of olive oil

2 Tsp. of Brain Octane Oil

2 Tsp. apple cider vinegar

Directions:

• Heat the oven up to 300 degrees Fahrenheit.

• Cut each of the spaghetti squash from one end to another, and remove the seeds and extraneous pulp. Pour a healthy dose of avocado oil and Himalayan salt over the squashes, and then put the combination into the oven for about 45 minutes.

• Check if it is done by piercing the pulp of the squash with a fork until it gets to the innermost part of the squash's skin.

• Use a round biscuit cutter to notch out a third of each of the spaghetti squash, and then place them into the oven for about 10 minutes.

• In a pot, heat 2 quarts of water gently until it boils, and add a dash of rice vinegar to it.

• Break one of the eggs into a small bowl, and then transfer it into the simmering water.

• Allow it to cook for about 3 minutes before taking it out.

• Repeat the same process for the second egg.

• Take out the squash from the oven.

• Use a fork to mash the avocado into a pulp, and then place the mixture into the biscuit cutter, right on the squash.

• With the aim of having the avocado at the bottom, flip the biscuit cutter over. Afterward, top with the poached egg, salt, olive oil and Brain Octane.

BACON AND EGG MUFFINS

This is one delicious meal for breakfast that you can prepare with ease, as it not only takes advantage of eggs and some tasty bacon but you can throw in some veggies, sausage, spices and herbs if you want to be adventurous and try out new things. Additionally, this gluten free egg muffins can be put in storage in the refrigerator so that they come in handy when you are feeling hungry or want to go on a trip.

Cook Time: 1 hour

Prep Time: 20 mins

Serves: 6

Ingredients:

5 eggs

1/4 tsp. unrefined salt

Some grinded fresh black pepper

1/4 Tsp. garlic powder

1/2 Tsp. coconut oil

2 cups spinach, chopped

3 strips of cooked bacon, cut into small pieces

1 Tbsp. fresh herbs, finely chopped parsley

Directions:

• Heat the oven up to 350 degrees Fahrenheit.

• Place silicone liners into muffin pans, and oil the liners lightly with coconut oil.

• Place a skillet on the cooker and apply medium heat to it. Put some fat into it and then watch it melt. Add the chopped spinach and sauté it for a minute until it starts to shrivel. Put out the heat and add the already sliced bacon pieces and fresh herbs. Stir the mixture to combine them properly.

• Crack the eggs into a big bowl, and then add salt, pepper, and garlic powder. Beat the mixture thoroughly and then put it to one side.

• Scoop out the spinach/bacon mishmash into the muffin cups before pouring the whisked eggs mixture over them uniformly.

• Place muffin cups into the oven and bake for about 20 minutes.

ASPARAGUS BREAKFAST INSPIRED BY BACON AND EGG

This is another easy, quick-to-prepare breakfast that you can make in less than 20 minutes. Although it may look like a difficult meal to prepare at first, you will soon find out how easily this delicious meal can be prepared before you head out for your daily hustle.

Cook Time: 20 minutes

Prep Time: 5 mins

Serves: 2

Ingredients:

4 slices bacon, chopped

12 sprigs trimmed asparagus

4 pastured eggs

1 Tbsp. chopped fresh chives

½ Tsp. fine grain sea salt

1 Tsp. fresh ground pepper

¼ Tsp. fresh ground pepper

Directions:

• Trim the asparagus and get rid of the woody stem.

• Put the skillet on medium heat, add the sliced bacon, and then cook till it becomes crusty.

• Take out the pieces of bacon and leave the drippings.

• Stir in the asparagus into the skillet and allow it to cook for around 5 minutes or till it turns crispy tender. The length of the cooking time is based on the thickness of the asparagus.

• Crack all 4 eggs over the asparagus before sprinkling chives, salt and pepper over them.

• On a medium to low heat, sauté the mixture till the egg white are set, and the yolks becomes soft

• Throw in the bacon and serve fresh and hot!

EGG AND VEGETABLE STIR-FRY

This breakfast keto recipe is full of protein and veggies and is designed to whet your appetite every morning while ensuring that you remain satisfied for long.

Cook Time: 15 minutes

Prep Time: 5 mins

Serves: 1

Ingredients:

½ Tsp. Ghee

A handful of fresh vegetables like carrots, cauliflower, broccoli, green beans

2 Pastured eggs

Spices like mixed herbs, thyme, and black pepper

1 cup spinach

Directions:

• On a cutting board, chop all the veggies and put them into a big bowl. Chop the spinach separately and put it in a different bowl.

• While on medium heat, put the skillet on the cooker and add ghee to it.

• Throw in the veggies

• Add salt to taste

• Break eggs into a bowl, and then whip it thoroughly

• Pour the whipped egg into the mixture in the skillet

• Add the spices

• Add spinach to the mixture

• Stir-fry until the mixture is ready.

• Add a dash of black pepper to it.

EGG AND SAUSAGE INSPIRED BREAKFAST SKILLET

This is one heck of a meal that is filled with lots of balanced protein, fat, and low-carb keto options that will leave you full all through the morning. In this recipe, you will find eggs, sweet potatoes, sausage, cilantro and avocado competing for space in the skillet.

Cook Time: 45 minutes

Prep Time: 15 mins

Serves: 2

Ingredients:

½ lb. breakfast sausage

1 medium sweet potatoes, diced

3 eggs, pasture raised

½ avocado, diced

Handful cilantro

Hot sauce

Raw cheese

Salt and pepper

Directions:

• Heat the oven up to 400 degrees Fahrenheit

• Place skillet over medium heat, and then transfer the sausage to it until it crumbles and become brown.

• As soon as it becomes brown, take it out and make sure you preserve enough of its fat to cook the sweet potatoes.

• Add the sweet potatoes to the sausage fat and allow them to cook very well until they become crusty.

• Put the sausage back into the skillet.

• Create space in the skillet that will hold each of the egg. Crack the eggs directly into the space.

• Put the skillet in the oven and bake the mixture for around 5 minutes or until the heat lets the eggs to set.

• Set the oven to broil so that it heats the topmost side of the eggs for some minutes. Except if you want the yolks to be runny, you should avoid letting it cook all through. But if you opt for the former option, then the runny yolks would perfectly go well with the crusty sweet potatoes.

• Take the skillet out of the oven and then cover the entire mixture with avocado, cilantro and hot sauce.

• When serving, use a big spoon to scoop out an egg and the surrounding goodies along with it!

SPINACH MUSHROOM AND FETA CRUSTLESS QUICHE

This low-carb breakfast is free of gluten, low in carbohydrate and will give your taste buds an incredible kick. Besides, it is full of veggies that will see you through the rigors of the morning exertions at your workplace.

Cook Time: 1 hour

Prep Time: 10 mins

Serves: 3

Ingredients:

4 oz. button mushrooms

½ clove garlic, minced

5 oz. box frozen spinach, thawed

2 pastured eggs

½ cup of milk

1 oz. feta cheese

½ Tsp. of coconut oil

¼ cup Parmesan cheese, grated

¼ cup shredded mozzarella

Unrefined Salt and pepper to taste

Directions:

• Heat the oven up to 350 degrees Fahrenheit

• Prepare the ingredients by washing the mushrooms and cutting them into thin slices. Next, remove excess moisture from the thawed spinach. Afterward, chop the garlic finely.

• While on medium heat, place a skillet on the cooker and then add some coconut oil to it.

• Throw mushrooms and garlic into the skillet. Sauté the mixture for around 7 minutes or till the mushrooms become soft, and all the moisture have vaporized.

• Grease the inner part of a 9-inch pie dish with non-stick spray. Set the already dried spinach at the base of the pie dish. Next, place the mushrooms on it, and on the next layer, put the crumbled feta cheese on the mushrooms.

• Crack the eggs into a fairly-sized bowl, and then add milk and Parmesan cheese. Whip the mixture thoroughly.

• Transfer the egg combination into the pie dish, over the veggies and feta cheese.

• Lastly, top everything with shredded mozzarella cheese.

• Set the pie dish on a baking sheet to enable movement back and forth the oven.

• Allow the crustless quiche to bake for around 50 minutes or till it becomes golden brown on the top.

• Cut and serve.

GRILLED SPICED CHICKEN WITH SALSA

If you are the type of individual that loves eating spiced chicken right off the bone, then this recipe will suit you quite fine. Not only does this recipe meet keto requirements, but it is going to be a favorite for the kids as well.

Cook Time: 45 hour

Prep Time: 5 mins

Serves: 2

Ingredients:

4 Chicken wings

Spices

Greens

Salsa

Directions:

Put the spices in a medium-sized bowl, and coat the chicken wings all over with the spice.

• Put the combination into the oven, and apply heat between 360-395 degrees Fahrenheit for around 40 minutes.

• Chicken wings should be served hot with greens and salsa.

BAKED AVOCADOS WITH SMOKED SALMON AND EGG FILLINGS

Not only is this meal loaded with sufficient protein and fats that will drive hunger pangs away for long but it is keto balanced and healthy too.

Cook Time: 20 mins

Prep Time: 5 mins

Serves: 2

Ingredients:

2 avocados

2 oz. smoked salmon

4 eggs, pasture raised

Unrefined Salt

Black pepper

Chili flakes

Fresh dilli

Directions:

• Heat the oven up to 425 degrees Fahrenheit.

• Split and remove the seeds from the avocados. Next, make a hole inside it, so that it is sufficient enough to hold an egg.

• Place the avocado halves on a cookie sheet and put some smoked salmon inside the hole.

• Crack the eggs into a small bowl, and then move the yolks and as much egg white the hole inside the avocados can hold.

• On the eggs, sprinkle some dash of black pepper and unrefined salt to taste.

• Arrange the cookie sheet in the oven and leave it for about 20 minutes.

• Dust some chili flakes and fresh dilli on the top of the avocado

• Serve avocados piping hot.

CHICKEN MEAT BAGELS

The flavor of chicken meat bagels is designed for your early morning enjoyment because the spices and other ingredients bring the taste to the fore profoundly.

Cook Time: 50 mins

Prep Time: 15 mins

Serve: 3

Ingredients:

¾ onions, finely diced

½ Tbsp. of ghee

1 pound of ground Chicken

1 big pastured egg

1/3 cup tomato sauce

½ Tsp. paprika

½ Tsp. sea salt

¼ Tsp. ground pepper

Directions:

• Heat the oven up to 400 degrees Fahrenheit.

• Line a baking dish with parchment paper.

• Over medium heat, add ghee to a skillet and then throw in the onions. Sauté the mixture until the onions become translucent. Let onions cool before using them again.

• In a fairly big bowl, add all the ingredients together including the chicken meat and onions. Combine them thoroughly so that the spices are distributed uniformly.

• Split the meat into six portions. Roll each portion into a ball with your hand, and then dent a hole in the middle. Next, shape it a little with your hands to give it a flat appearance and make it look more like a bagel.

• Once you're through, set it aside on a plate, and then repeat the process with the remaining portions of spiced chicken meat.

• Arrange them in an oven and bake until the bagel-like meat is completely cooked (around 40 minutes).

• Remove the meat bagel from the oven and let it cool. Cut it as you'd normally slice a regular bagel.

• Place healthy greens of your choice like onions, tomato slices, lettuce in between the meat bagel and then serve them.

BACON AND EGGS

If you have been working out regularly, this low carbohydrate meal will help you up your fat and protein intake as it is loaded with both nutrients. Besides, the pork cuts, eggs, and avocado make a perfect combination for breakfast.

Cook Time: 5 mins

Prep Time: 10 mins

Serves: 1

Ingredients:

½ Tbsp. ghee

2 eggs

2 oz. sirloin

1/4 avocado

Unrefined salt

Pepper

Directions:

• While on medium heat, place pan on the cooker and add ghee.

• Crack the eggs into the pan, and allow them to fry until the egg whites are set and the yolks get done to your preference.

• Sprinkle a dash of pepper and salt over the mixture.

• Place bacon into another pan and cook until it gets done to your preference. Afterward, cut them into bite-sized strips and add salt and pepper to taste.

• Cut up some avocado and serve them together!

BACON MEAT AND EGG BALLS

Delicious bacon meat and eggs, all rolled into balls, are the ideal breakfast meals that will see you through the morning while conquering any form of craving that could arise along the way.

Cook Time: 45 mins

Prep Time: 10 mins

Serves: 3

Ingredients:

2 large eggs, pastured

1/4 cup ghee, softened at room temperature

1 Tbsp. mayonnaise

Black pepper, freshly ground

1/4 Tsp. unrefined salt

2 large slices of bacon

Directions:

- Heat the oven up to 375 degrees Fahrenheit.

- Line a baking tray with baking paper.

- Arrange the strips of bacon on the baking paper while ensuring that there is enough space for them not to overlap.

- Set the tray in the oven and bake for around 15 minutes or until the bacon turns golden brown. Cooking time should be based on the thickness of the bacon cuts.

- Once they are done, take them away from the oven and put them to one side. Allow them to cool.

- Fill a pan with water and place the eggs into it. Add some salt to stop them from cracking.

- Apply heat to the pan for around 10 minutes and for the eggs to become hard-boiled.

- Once they are done, use a spoon to take out the eggs, and then put them into a bowl of cold water. Peel and quarter them as soon as they become cool.

- Add the quartered eggs to pieces of butter and then mash the mixture with a fork.

- Drizzle fat from the bacon over mixture; and for seasoning, throw in some dash of salt and pepper along with mayonnaise. Combine mixture thoroughly.

- Put the mixture into the refrigerator for around 30 minutes or till it becomes solid enough to form the balls.

- Crush the bacon into small pieces and get them ready for "breading." Take out the egg mixture from the refrigerator and start to form the balls. Make use of a spoon to roll each ball in the bacon crumbles, and arrange them on a tray that will go into the refrigerator.

BROCCOLI AND EGG BREAKFAST

This is the sort of breakfast that you can make quickly and easily, especially when you don't have time to cook or you are just too lazy to do anything in the kitchen. Besides, you don't have to be adept at cooking before you can pull this recipe off. Your choice of proteins could come in the form of spiced bacon, minced meat or chicken, while fried egg or avocado as toppings would be apt.

Cook Time: 25 mins

Prep Time: 10 mins

Serves: 2

Ingredients:

2 medium Broccoli

4 slices bacon

1 small white onion

3 garlic cloves

2 Tbsp. coconut oil

2 Tbsp. freshly chopped parsley or chives

½ Tsp. Unrefined salt

2 large pastured egg

Directions:

• Cut the bacon into small slices. Next, peel the onion bulbs and garlic and chop them finely.

• Place a skillet on the cooker and apply medium heat to it. Throw in the bacon, chopped onions, and garlic.

• Sautee mixture by stirring them repeatedly until they are cooked and lightly browned.

• Chop the broccoli into medium pieces.

• Throw the broccoli into the mixture in the pan and cook for some minutes.

• As soon as it is done, remove skillet away from the cooker and add chopped parsley to the combination.

• Top with a fried egg.

• Serve.

CREAM CHEESE PANCAKES

The cream cheese pancakes are an excellent substitute to the regular dough-based pancakes and serve as a delicious and satisfying breakfast that is quick and easy to make since the batter can be prepared in a couple of minutes.

Cook Time: 10 mins

Prep Time: 5 mins

Serves: 2

Ingredients:

4 oz. cream cheese

4 eggs

2 Tsp. Stevia

1 Tsp. cinnamon

Instructions:

• Add cream cheese, eggs, stevia, and cinnamon into a food processor and pulse on high until it reaches a smooth consistency.

• Allow mixture to rest and bubbles to settle for around 2 minutes.

• Grease frying pan with a spray of coconut oil and place it on a cooker that is set to medium heat.

• Transfer about ¼ of batter into the hot pan and cook for about 2 minutes until it turns golden. Flip it over and cook the other side for another one minute.

• Repeat the process with the remaining batter.

• Before serving, you may drizzle any sugar-free syrup that is keto-approved over them.

CHAPTER NINE: SNACKS

In general, snacks should have a balance of healthy fats, protein, and some carbs. While the three macronutrients do not have to be in the perfect proportion, you may still enjoy a snack having a combination of any two of the three. But try as much as possible to avoid snacking on pure carbohydrates alone. Fats and protein are to make you feel full and to stop yearnings and hunger pains from overwhelming you. Raw green veggies are also a great option if you are to take them as snacks. In this chapter, you will find great snack recipes that you can even make with ease.

ALMONDS MAKE HEALTHY KETO SNACKS

BACON CHIPS AND GUACAMOLE DIP

This is the perfect snack for watching your favorite movie, and it is loaded with some fat and protein goodies that will leave you longing for more. Quality pork is essential for you to be able to get bacon slices that do not crumble when dipped into the guacamole. The guacamole, itself, is spiced up with some herbs that enhance its tastes considerably.

Cook Time: 20 mins

Prep Time: 10 mins

Serves: 2

Ingredients:

4 strips thick-cut, bacon

1 avocado

¼ cup red onion,

½ Tbsp. cilantro,

½ Tbsp. jalapeño, minced

¼ Tsp. ground cumin

¼ Tsp. pink Himalayan salt

Directions:

• Heat the oven up to 375 degrees Fahrenheit.

• Line a baking sheet with parchment paper.

• One after the other, cut the bacon strips into 3 pieces each and places them on the baking sheet.

• Place it in the oven and bake for about 20 minutes.

• Take out the bacon from the oven and let them crisp up in a small bowl.

• Use a fork to mash the avocados in a small bowl.

• Add red onion, jalapeño, ground cumin and Himalayan salt

• Serve the bacon chips together with the guacamole dip.

SPICY AVOCADO HUMMUS

You can prepare the spicy avocado hummus in a relatively short time. This is a breakfast meal that goes well as dipping for chopped veggies.

Cook Time: 0 mins

Prep Time: 10 mins

Serves: 4

Ingredients:

2 cups canned chickpeas, rinsed and drained

¼ cup freshly squeezed lemon juice

⅓ cup extra-virgin olive oil

½ avocado, halved, pitted and peeled

1 ½ Tbsp. tahini

½ jalapeño, chopped

½ garlic clove

Himalayan pink salt

Black pepper, freshly ground

Pinch of cayenne pepper

Chopped green vegetables of your choice for dipping

Directions:

• Put chickpeas, lemon juice, olive oil, avocado, tahini, jalapeño and garlic into the food processor and pulse on high speed until everything becomes smooth.

• Add salt and black pepper.

• Sprinkle cayenne pepper over the mixture

• Serve with your choice of veggies.

HUMMUS DEVILED EGG

This recipe is another inventive way of making the deviled eggs. It is designed to provide you with sufficient protein — in the form of chickpeas and the egg yolks.

Cook Time: 0 mins

Prep Time: 10 mins

Yields: 10 deviled eggs

Ingredients:

5 large eggs

½ can chickpeas, rinsed and drained

½ clove garlic, peeled, chopped

2 Tbsp. fresh lemon juice

½ Tsp. coconut aminos

1 ½ Tbsp. vegetable broth

⅛ paprika for garnish

¼ Tsp Himalayan pink salt for garnish

Directions:

• Fill a medium-sized saucepan with water up to 2 inches, and then put the eggs inside.

• Apply high heat to the saucepan for about 13 minutes or until it boils.

• Get a bowl of ice water ready and let it remain cool.

• Put the cooker off. Allow the eggs to cool in the saucepan by letting it stay untouched for about 14 minutes.

• Using a slotted spoon, take the eggs out and drop them into the bowl of ice water.

• Let the eggs cool for about 10 minutes.

• As soon as they become cool, take out the egg shell and slice the eggs into two from end-to-end. Remove the yolks and keep them separately. Do the same thing with the rest of the eggs.

• Put all the yolks along with chickpeas, garlic, lemon juice, coconut aminos, and vegetable broth into a food processor and pulse on high-speed until you get a thick smooth consistency.

• Pour the yolk mixture into a piping bag, and pipe in the mixture into the hollow portion of the egg white.

• For the garnish, sprinkle paprika and some dash of Himalayan salt on them.

KETO PROTEIN BAR

This keto protein bars pack a lot of healthy fat and protein just for your enjoyment!

Cook Time: 1 hour, 10 mins

Prep Time: 10 mins

Serves: 4

Ingredients:

½ cup of almond butter

2 Tbsps. of coconut oil (melted)

1 scoop of vanilla protein

½ Tsp. of powdered stevia

¼ Tsp. of Himalayan salt

2 Tbsps. of sugar-free chocolate chips

½ Tsp. of cinnamon

Directions:

• Combine all the ingredients together and transfer them into a baking dish.

• Place the baking dish into the freezer till they become firm.

• Slice them into bars

• You may choose to put the protein bars in the refrigerator until it is time for you to relish the taste of these amazing snacks!

COCONUT PROTEIN COOKIES

Cook Time: 30 mins

Prep Time: 15 mins

Yields: 10 cookies

Ingredients:

1 ½ cups shredded coconut flakes

¼ cup sunflower seeds

¼ cup fine protein powder

5-7 drops of liquid stevia

½ Tsp. of vanilla

½ Tsp. cinnamon

½ Tbsps. coconut oil

1/8 cup filtered water

Directions:

- Heat the oven up to 300 degrees Fahrenheit.

- Put the sunflower seeds into a food processor and pulse on low until they are broken into pieces.

- Put all the ingredients into a medium bowl and mix together thoroughly. Should the mixture turns out to be too crumbly, then add some coconut oil and perhaps more water.

- Scoop the batter into the cookie tray.

- Lightly press the cookies down to flatten them. Make your desired number of cookies (ten in this case).

- Place cookie tray into oven and bake for around 15 minutes.

- Serve.

CHOCOLATE MUFFINS

When you get the urge to satisfy the cravings that a sweet tooth normally brings, these low-carb muffins will surely be available to help you indulge in a unique keto treat. Aside from the ingredients being readily available, they are easy to make and at a quick rate too.

Cook Time: 12 mins

Prep Time: 10 mins

Yields: 9 muffins

Ingredients:

½ cup natural creamy almond butter

1/3 cup confectioner's erythritol

1 Tbsp. unsweetened cocoa powder

1 Tbsp. peanut butter powder

1 large pastured egg

½ Tbsp. dairy-free melted salted butter

1 Tbsp. water

¾ Tsp. pure vanilla extract

½ Tsp. baking soda

1/8 cup sugar-free dark chocolate baking chips.

Directions:

• Heat the oven up to 350 degrees Fahrenheit.

• Cover a rimmed baking sheet with silicone mini muffin pan

• With the exception of the dark chocolate baking chips, put the rest of the ingredients into a big mixing bowl. By means of an electric hand mixer, combine all the ingredients thoroughly until you have a smooth consistency (the dough must be somewhat thick).

• Fill 9 of the wells of the mini muffin pan with the batter.

• Place the baking sheet in the oven and bake for about 11 minutes.

• Take out the baking sheet from the oven and arrange it on a cooling rack to let the muffins lose some steam before serving them.

MARINATED OLIVES

This recipe will let you enjoy olives that have been spiced with orange zest, fennel seed, and pepper flakes.

Cook Time: 5 mins

Prep Time: 10 mins

Yields: 2

Ingredients:

2 oranges

8 cloves garlic, peeled

½ Tsp. fennel seed

Crushed red pepper flakes to taste

½ cup extra-virgin olive oil

2 cup assorted olives with pits

Directions:

• By employing the use of a vegetable peeler, take out the orange zest and ensure that you get some long strands while avoiding the white pith at the same time.

• Cut the long strand into 2 inch strands. Roll one strand into a tight coil, then cut from corner to corner to make long thin strips.

• Chop the garlic finely.

• Place a small skillet on high heat and add the garlic, orange strands, fennel seed, crushed red pepper flakes and olive oil.

• Reduce the heat to low and let the mixture simmer for around 3 minutes.

• Be vigilant and avoid letting the garlic to become brown. Take the skillet away from the heat if you'll have to ensure that it doesn't.

• Put the olives in a bowl and drizzle the marinade over it. Allow it to sit for no less than one hour and at room temperature before serving or storing.

• Prior to serving, you need to bring olives to room temperature.

KETO ONION RINGS

Cook Time: 15 mins

Prep Time: 15 mins

Serves: 4

Ingredients:

2 medium white onions

1 cup Coconut flour

4 large pastured eggs

2 Tbsp. Heavy Whipping Cream

4 oz. Pork Rinds

1 cup grated parmesan cheese

Directions:

• Slice the onions across its width so that you get half inch thick rings.

• Break rings into pieces and separate all the inside pieces that you don't need.

• Use separate bowls to create different coating stations for egg wash, coconut flour, heavy whipping cream, and pork rind parmesan.

• Begin the process by coating the onion ring in the coconut flour, and then run it through the rest of the stations before placing it on a baking rack. .

• As soon as you are through with the first coating, repeat processes by recoating them all over, beginning with the egg wash.

• Arrange the double-coated rings on an oiled baking rack.

• Heat up the oven up to 425 degrees Fahrenheit.

• Place the baking rack into the oven and bake for about 15 minutes

• Serve piping hot and enjoy!

CHAPTER TEN: DINNER

Making dinner after a very hectic day can be very challenging, especially when you have to take into account the duration and difficulty involved in cooking regular dinners. Most of the recipes in this chapter are keto-compliant, easy-to-cook and are intended to give your taste bud a massive kick!

A KETO DINNER

KETO BEEF STIR FRY

Cook Time: 15 mins

Prep Time: 10 mins

Serves: 4

Ingredients:

1 cup zucchini, spiralized into 6-inch noodles

2 bunch baby bok choy

½ cup organic broccoli florets

16 ounces grass-fed flank, sliced into thin strips

Two Knobs of ginger, peeled and sliced into thin strips

4 Tbsp. ghee, divided

2 Tsp. coconut aminos

Directions:

• Prepare the bok choy by cutting off the end of its stem and getting rid of them.

• Apply high heat to a pan, and then add a little ghee. Sear both sides of the steak for about 2 minutes.

• Reduce the heat to medium, and add some more ghee. Throw in broccoli, ginger and coconut aminos.

• Allow mixture to cook for a minute, even as you continue to stir repeatedly.

• Add bok choy and let the mixture cook for an extra one minute.

• Add zucchini to the mixture and let everything boil to your preferred liking. But pay attention because they cook very rapidly.

LOW-CARB BAKED SALMON

You can pull off this recipe with few healthy ingredients and at a quick rate too. But you must bear in mind that a high-quality salmon is imperative for the success of this meal.

Cook Time: 5 mins

Prep Time: 20 mins

Serves: 2

Ingredients:

2/3 pound wild Coho salmon

1 Tbsp. lemon juice

1 clove garlic, minced

1 Tbsp. cold butter, cubed

¼ Tsp. salt

1/8 Tsp. black pepper

1/8 Tsp. Italian seasoning

1/8 Tsp. red pepper flakes

½ Tbsp. parsley, chopped

Directions:

• Set a rack in the center of the oven and heat it up to 350 degrees Fahrenheit.

• Apply medium heat to a pan, and stir in the minced garlic and some lemon juice.

• Add a tablespoon of butter into the mixture and take the pan away from the cooker. Twirl the mixture so that the butter begins to melt.

• Put the pan back on the cooker and heat mixture for some seconds. Remove mixture again and keep on swirling until the butter totally melts.

• Add a second tablespoon of butter, and repeat the process again. As soon as the butter melts fully, take the pan away from the cooker.

• Get a piece of foil to hold the salmon filet, and with sufficient room to fold down and seal.

• Brush the salmon filet with the garlic butter sauce by making use of a brush.

• Add seasoning like salt, pepper, Italian seasoning, and red pepper flakes. Seal the sides well with foil so that the sauce doesn't seep out.

• With the salmon wrapped inside, place the foil into the oven, and then bake for about 14 minutes or till it becomes firm. With the foil opened, let the salmon to broil for about 3 minutes while ensuring that it doesn't burn.

• Remove from the oven.

• Garnish baked salmon with parsley, and serve instantly!

CRACK SLAW EGG ROLL

Like most meals in this chapter, the ingredients for the crack slaw egg roll are not hard to get and can be cooked in a short time as well.

Cook Time: 15 mins

Prep Time: 15 mins

Serves: 3

Ingredients:

½ Tbsp. Avocado oil

2 cloves garlic, minced

1½ Tbsp. fresh ginger, minced

½ lb. grass-fed ground beef

½ Tsp. Sea salt

1/8 Tsp. Black pepper

½ lb. Shredded coleslaw mix

1/8 cup Coconut aminos

1 Tsp. Toasted sesame oil

1/8 cup Green onions

Directions:

• Place a large saucepan on the cooker and apply medium-high heat to it. Add some avocado oil to the pan. Afterward, throw in the minced garlic and ginger.

• Sauté mixture for around one minute, until fragrant.

• Put in the ground beef and seasonings like sea salt and black pepper.

• Allow mixture to cook for around 10 minutes or until it becomes brown.

• Adjust the heat to medium, and add the coleslaw mix and coconut aminos.

• Stir the mixture thoroughly and then cover the saucepan. Let it cook for around 5 minutes or till the cabbage is tender.

• Take the saucepan away from the heat.

• Add toasted sesame oil and green onions.

BRAZILIAN STEAK

The success of the Brazilian steak depends on utilizing the tender parts of the beef such as skirt steak and flap meat. This tasty Brazilian delight is a meal that is ideally suited for dinner, in particular, when you want something fast and easy to cook.

Ingredients:

Cook Time: 5 mins

Prep Time: 10 mins

Serves: 2

Ingredients:

3 cloves garlic, minced

Unrefined salt

¾ lb. flap meat, trimmed and cut into 2 pieces

Black pepper, freshly ground

1 Tbsp. ghee

1 oz. unsalted butter

½ Tbsp. parsley, chopped fresh

Directions:

• Add a dash of salt to the minced garlic.

• Pat the beef cuts dry and season all of its sides with salt and pepper very well.

• Place a skillet on the cooker and apply medium-high heat to it. Add ghee to it and leave it for a while until it starts to simmer.

• Put in the steak and let each side cook for around 3 minutes — for them to become brown.

• Put off the heat, and remove the steak from the skillet to another plate. Allow the steak to rest just as you prepare the garlic butter.

• Apply low-heat to a small skillet and then add butter to it. Put in the garlic and stir it repeatedly for around 4 minutes till it turns golden a little.

• Add a little salt to taste.

• Cut the steak, drizzle garlic butter over them, and garnish with parsley before serving!

LOW CARB FRITTATA

This frittata recipe brings the alluring power of vegetables, cheese, fresh herbs, and sausages to your taste buds. Aside from being very quick and easy to cook, you can use remnants of foods as part of your ingredients as well.

Cook Time: 5 mins

Prep Time: 10 mins

Serves: 4

Ingredients:

12 pastured eggs

1 medium-sized white onion, peeled and sliced

7.0 oz. cup feta cheese, crumbled

7.0 oz. cup cherry tomatoes, halved

2 Tbsp. ghee

4 Tbsp. herbs basil, freshly chopped

Himalayan pink salt

Black pepper, freshly ground

Directions:

• Heat the oven up to 400 degrees Fahrenheit.

• Apply medium heat to a pan greased with ghee. Add the sliced onion and let it cook until it becomes brown.

• Crack the eggs into a medium-sized bowl, and season with salt and pepper, and the finely basil. Beat the mixture thoroughly.

• The moment the onion turns brown, pour in the eggs till the edges begin to turn opaque

• Use the crumbled cheese and halved cherry tomatoes as toppings.

• Position the mixture under the broiler and cook for around 7 minutes or when it is cooked at the top.

• Take away the pan from the oven and allow the mixture to cool.

• Serve frittata right away or store it in the refrigerator for about 5 days.

GARLIC SCALLOPS

Scallops are rich in vitamins, vital minerals, omega-3 fatty acids and lean protein among several others. This recipe has scallops as the base while ghee, garlic and a drizzle of fresh lemon are designed to give it some sparks.

Cook Time: 5 mins

Prep Time: 5 mins

Serves: 4

Ingredients:

2 lb. large scallops

½ Cup clarified butter ghee

10 cloves garlic, grated

2 large lemons, zested

½ Cup Italian parsley, roughly chopped

1 Tsp. sea salt

½ Tsp. peppercorn medley, freshly ground

½ Tsp. red pepper flakes

A pinch of sweet paprika

1 Tsp. extra virgin olive oil

Directions:

• Prior to cooking the scallops, ensure that you pat them dry with paper towels.

• Apply medium heat to a large cast iron skillet.

• In the meantime, drizzle butter ghee over the scallops in a medium bowl. The butter ghee should be sufficient enough to cover them completely. Season the mixture by tossing in sea salt, cracked red pepper flakes, and sweet paprika just enough to coat the scallops lightly.

• Pour in some butter ghee to the searing skillet so that it coats the bottom. Begin to add the scallops but ensure that the pan isn't overcrowded. Cook both sides for around 2 minutes until they turn golden —a small spatula for flipping them over should suffice here.

• Put the butter ghee and then garlic into the skillet. Take the mixture away from the cooker, and use a spatula to stir the garlic around for about 30 seconds so that it can permeate the sauce properly. The heat coming off the skillet will aid the garlic in weaving its magic into the butter. This aspect is essential as it prevents the mixture from having an undesirable pungent burnt garlicky taste — in fact, it is the best way to draw out the sweetness of garlic without having any burning.

• Drizzle half of the lemon juice over the mixture and physically move the skillet around a bit so that it mixes well with the butter.

• Add a healthy dose of minced parsley, lemon zest and a sprinkle of extra virgin olive oil.

• You may choose to serve with crusty bread.

KETO EGGPLANT CHIPS

This recipe has the eggplant as its base and is easy to make for a memorable spicy dinner.

Cook Time: 5 mins

Prep Time: 45 mins

Serves: 8

Ingredients:

2 medium eggplants

Kosher salt

4 Tbsp. extra-virgin olive oil

½ Cup freshly grated Parmesan

2 Tsp. Italian seasoning

2 Tsp. garlic powder

Black pepper, freshly ground

Marinara, for dipping

Directions:

• Heat the oven up to 350 degrees Fahrenheit.

• Slice eggplants into extremely thin rounds.

• Arrange the slices on paper towels in an even layer.

• Add a little salt, and allow it to sit for about 10 minutes.

• Use a paper towel to clean up any moisture that builds up on the slices, and then flip over.

• Once more, salt, rest and dry the eggplants again just like before.

• Move all the eggplant slices to a big bowl and drizzle oil over them. Afterward, put in the Parmesan cheese, garlic powder, and Italian seasoning.

• Add a dash of black pepper to the eggplant slices, and toss mixture until they are coated evenly.

• On a large baking sheet, place the slices in an even layer while ensuring that they do not overlap.

• Place it in the oven and bake for about 18 minutes or until you get a golden and crispy eggplant.

• Serve with marinara after it has cooled down.

CHAPTER ELEVEN: MAINS

Mains can be defined as the principal dish of a meal and is the basis around which the meal is built. It could be fish, chicken, meat, etc., and usually goes along with one or more side dishes — which, themselves are designed to go together with the main dish. Find below, some great keto main dishes that you can enjoy with other meals.

MAINS

KETO ROASTED CHICKEN

This is a unique opportunity for you to make your own roasted chicken. Just keep in mind that to get a tasty and well-roasted chicken, a read thermometer should be available so that you can take it out of the oven when the temperature hits around 165^0C.

Cook Time: 1 hour 20 mins

Prep Time: 15 mins

Serves: 4

Ingredients:

1 whole pasture-raised chicken with insides removed

9 sprigs of fresh thyme

Herbs like thyme, rosemary, basil,

2 Tsp. Himalayan salt

½ Tsp. pepper, freshly ground

1 lemon, halved

5 cloves garlic

2 Tbsp. olive oil

Directions:

• Heat the oven up to 450 degrees Fahrenheit.

• Let loose the skin around the breast region of the chicken, and spice up the area underneath the skin with seasonings that you like — here, some thyme, salt, etc., should suffice.

• Season the chicken in and out with salt and pepper.

• Put in the remaining thyme, salt, garlic, lemon, and other seasonings into the cavity of the chicken.

• Tressing the chicken would help seal up the chicken cavity, and hold the juices together while cooking,

• Set the chicken on a medium-size roasting pan and drizzle olive oil lightly on the entire arrangement —.chicken and roasting pan.

• Allow chicken to roast till a meat thermometer placed in the thickest part of the thigh gives a reading of 165^0C, usually around 45 minutes to an hour.

• As soon as it has reached the required level of doneness, take it out of the oven.

• Allow it to stand for 15 minutes before serving.

KETO SHREDDED CHICKEN

Cook Time: 2 hours

Prep Time: 10 mins

Serves: 3

Ingredients

¾ lbs. chicken boneless thighs

1 Tbsp. ghee

2 peppers Chipotle peppers in Adobo sauce

½ Tsp. Himalayan Pink Salt

1 Tsp. Oregano

¼ Tsp. Cumin

¼ Tsp. Cayenne Pepper

½ Medium shallots

2 cloves garlic

¼ lime juice

Water

Directions:

• Place a cast iron skillet on a cooker, and apply medium heat to it. Next, add ghee to the skillet.

• As soon as the ghee heats up, put in the chicken thighs. Allow the chicken thighs to turn brown on both sides.

• Put the Chipotle peppers in Adobo sauce, salt, oregano, cumin, cayenne pepper, shallot, garlic, lime juice, and water into a food processor. Pulse on high-speed until all the ingredients become smooth and consistent.

• As soon as the chicken thighs in the skillet turn brown to your desire, stir in the sauce over them. Cook the mixture for about 90 minutes, while turning the chicken thighs over from time to time. Should the volume of the sauce go down, keep on adding water to bring it back to its previous level.

• Use a fork and tongs to shred the chicken while it is still in the pan and after cooking for one and half hour. But if you find it hard to separate the meat from the bones inside the pan, then you'll have to take them out and use a knife. Afterward, put the shredded pieces back into the pan to cook further.

• Allow the shredded chicken to simmer for 30 minutes.

• After that, let the volume of the sauce to go down one last time while ensuring that it doesn't get burnt if it decreases too much.

• Serve after garnishing with lime and cilantro!

COCONUT CURRY CHICKEN

You will savor the taste of this chicken curry which has been soaked in the flavor of healthy spices, and coconut milk.

Cook Time: 1 hour

Prep Time: 20 mins

Serves: 3

Ingredients:

3 Raw Boneless chicken thighs

½ Can Coconut Milk

½ Cup chicken broth

1 ¼ Tbsp. coconut oil

½ Tbsp. curry powder

2 Cloves garlic

½ Tsp. grated ginger

½ Tsp. ground cinnamon

½ Tsp. Pink Salt

¼ Medium Red Onions

Directions:

• Cut the onion and garlic into fine pieces, and then grate the ginger root. Next, cut the chicken into 1-inch cubes.

• Place a fairly large skillet on a cooker and apply medium-high heat. Add coconut oil to the skillet and allow it to heat up.

• Put the boneless chicken thighs into the searing coconut oil and cook partially.

• Throw in the onion, ginger, garlic, curry powder, and cinnamon into the skillet holding the chicken thighs, and cook for about 3 minutes. Make sure you don't burn the spices!

• Pour in the coconut milk and chicken broth and stir.

• Cook for about an hour until the mixture gives you a preferred uniformity. By then, the sauce ought to be sufficiently thick, but if it is not, then allow it to cook further.

BAKED CHICKEN WINGS

Not only is this delicious baked chicken wings easy to cook, but the influence of key ingredients like butter, garlic, and Parmesan cheese gives the meal an entirely new twist that will make you ask for more!

Cook Time: 50 hours

Prep Time: 10 mins

Serves: 4

Ingredients:

Wings

2 lb. Chicken Wings

2 Tbsp. Baking powder

2 Tsp. Himalayan Pink Salt

GARLIC PARMESAN

8 slices thick cut bacon

4 Tbsp. bacon grease

8 Tbsp. Butter

4 Tsp. garlic

½ cup grated parmesan cheese

½ cup fresh parsley, chopped

½ Tsp. Himalayan Pink Salt

½ Tsp. black pepper

Directions:

• Heat the oven up to 250 degrees Fahrenheit.

• Pat the chicken wings dry, and put them into a Ziploc bag.

• Throw in some salt and baking powder into the bag and then shake vigorously until the wings are well-coated.

• Arrange them evenly on a baking rack that is set on a baking sheet before putting them into the oven for about 20 minutes.

• Increase the heat to 450^0C and cook for an extra 30 minutes until chicken wings are brown and crusty.

• Chop each slice of bacon into three equal parts. Put them in a skillet and cook. Set them aside.

• In a small pan, add bacon drippings and butter, and then apply heat to the mixture until the butter melts. Sprinkle salt and pepper to taste. Stir mixture and then take it away from the heat.

• Scoop out the cooked wings and bacon strips into a big Tupperware.

• Put parsley and Parmesan cheese on the mixture

• Drizzle the butter sauce over the chicken wings and bacon mixture. Cover the lid of the Tupperware and shake vigorously until they are well combined.

• Serve right away!

CHAPTER TWELVE:
DESSERTS, SIDES, SALADS, AND SOUPS

A dessert is a food that brings dinner to an end. They are often made up of fruity or sweet foods like confections dishes or fruit. While beverages like liquor or dessert wine can be used as desserts in a conventional setting, they are not allowed in a ketogenic diet. In this chapter, you will find easy-to-make dessert recipes when you are on a keto diet.

DESSERT

CINNAMON ROLLS

Not only are these cinnamon rolls easy to make, they are free of sugar and grain, and will give your ketosis an incredible boost!

Cook Time: 35 mins

Prep Time: 15 mins

Serves: 4

Ingredients:

For the Dough:

3/8 cup almond flour

½ Tbsp. baking powder

7/8 cup shredded mozzarella cheese

1 Tbsp. cream cheese

1 large pastured egg

¼ Tsp. vanilla extract

1/8 cup sugar-free sweetener

For the Rolls:

1/6 cup sugar-free sweetener

1/8 cup melted butter

1 Tsp. ground cinnamon

For the Icing:

3 oz. cream cheese, softened

½ Tbsp. whipping cream

½ Tsp. water

½ Tsp. sugar-free sweetener

Directions:

• Heat the oven up to 375 degrees Fahrenheit.

• In a microwave safe bowl, add almond flour, baking powder, and mozzarella cheese and mix properly.

• Put in cream cheese and cook in the microwave for a minute. Put off the machine; stir the mixture and then cook for an extra 30 seconds.

• Add egg, vanilla, and sweetener, and mix thoroughly, until the dough begins to form.

• Putting batter in the fridge for around 15 minutes allows it to firm and dry off the dough a bit

• Lightly apply coconut oil to parchment paper to prevent sticking from occurring and put the dough in between two of such papers.

• Using a rolling pin, roll dough into a rectangular form until it is about ¼ inch thick.

• Drizzle melted butter over the top of the dough; next, sprinkling sugar-free sweetener over it, and then ground cinnamon.

• Roll dough into a tube by beginning from the long side. Use a knife to cut four 1-inch pinwheel slices.

• Lightly grease some pie pans, and move each slice into them. Leave enough room for the dough to rise in between each roll.

• Put pie pans into the oven and bake for about 30 minutes or till they turn golden brown and are cooked throughout. Take it out of the oven and then allow it cool a bit.

Icing:

• Using a hand mixer, mix all the ingredients. Use a teaspoon to spread them on each cinnamon roll.

• Serve!

PEANUT BUTTER

This is a great dessert to have after the main course of a meal and is keto-friendly and delicious too. Besides, you don't stand the risk of exceeding your calorie intake since the ingredients are really healthy too.

Cook Time: 10 mins

Prep Time: 10 mins

Yields: 16

Ingredients:

1 cup peanut butter, creamy, no added sugar

½ cup grass-fed whey protein powder with no sugar and vanilla added

½ cup peanut butter powder

½ cup erythritol, granular

Directions:

• Put cookie sheet to one side after lining it with parchment paper,

• In a medium mixing bowl, put all the ingredients and mix properly.

Here, a wooden spoon would be apt at for mixing at the early stage of blending. Afterward, use your hands to knead the dough into a uniform consistency.

• Prepare a cookie sheet and place the dough on it. Then split it into 12 equal portions. Roll each of them into a small ball of around 3/4" in diameter.

• Put the cookie sheet and its content into the freezer for no less than 30 minutes to set.

• Serve.

CHEESE PANCAKES WITH BERRIES

If the popular saying that "all the good things in life are free" is true, then you need to try out this delightful cheese pancakes topped with amazing berries!

Cook Time: 30 mins

Prep Time: 10 mins

Yields: 8

Ingredients:

8 pastured eggs

14 oz. cottage cheese

2 Tbsp. ground psyllium husk powder

4 oz. coconut oil

Toppings

1 cup fresh blueberries (or any berry of your choice)

2 cup heavy whipping cream

Directions:

• In a medium-sized bowl, put eggs, cottage cheese, and ground psyllium husk powder and combine them thoroughly.

• Allow mixture to sit and to become thick for about 10 minutes.

• Apply low-medium heat to a non-stick skillet on a cooker, and add some coconut oil to it. Allow coconut oil to warm up before transferring the batter into it.

• Fry pancakes on either side for around 3 minutes. Avoid making them too large as they will be difficult to flip over.

• In a separate bowl, put in the heavy whipping, and whip it until it forms soft peaks.

• Top the pancake with the whipped cream and serve with the blue-berries!

BANANA WAFFLES

Made with keto-compliant ingredients, these waffles are designed for you to start the day on a bright note, and to hit the ground running too!

Cook Time: 20 mins

Prep Time: 10 mins

Yields: 16

Ingredients:

2 ripe bananas

8 pastured eggs

1 ½ cup almond flour

1 ½ cup of coconut milk

2 Tbsp. ground psyllium husk powder

2 pinch salt

2 Tsp. baking powder

1 Tsp. vanilla extract

2 Tsp. ground cinnamon

Butter

Directions:

• In a medium-sized bowl, combine all the ingredients and allow it to sit for some time.

• Add butter to a pan and scoop in the mixture to make waffles.

• Top waffles with whipped coconut cream and serve with a few fresh berries.

SIDES

Often referred to as a *"side order,"* they usually go with the main course at a meal, and you will find some excellent sides that will suit your keto-genic diet below.

CREAMY GREEN BEANS

This is a creamed green beans side that will go very well with your favorite fish, meat and vegetable dishes.

Cook Time: 15 mins

Prep Time: 10 mins

Serves: 8

Ingredients:

20 oz. fresh green beans

6 oz. butter

1 Tsp. unrefined salt

½ Tsp. ground black pepper

2 cup heavy whipping cream

1 lemon, the zest

1 cup fresh parsley

Directions:

• Prepare the green beans by trimming and rinsing it.

• Apply heat to a frying pan on a cooker and put in some butter. Allow butter to heat up.

• Throw in the beans and sauté for about 4 minutes on medium-high heat until they start turning brown.

• Reduce the heat just before the end, and season with a dash of salt and pepper.

• Top the mixture with heavy cream and allow it to cook for 1-2 minutes.

• Before serving, add the zest of lemon and finely chopped parsley.

COLESLAW

This is a popular savory cabbage salad with healthy and keto-friendly ingredients that will make you ask for more!

Cook Time: 15 mins

Prep Time: 5 mins

Serves: 8

Ingredients:

1 lb. green cabbage

1 lemon, juiced

2 Tsp. salt

1 cup mayonnaise

2 pinch fennel seeds

2 pinch pepper

2 Tbsp. Dijon mustard

Directions:

• Core the cabbage and shred with a food processor.

• Put the cabbage into a medium-sized bowl.

• Sprinkle a dash of salt and lemon juice on it.

• Mix very well for ingredients to combine. Leave it for about 10 minutes for the cabbage to wilt a little. Get rid of any excess liquid.

• Add mayonnaise and mustard to the combination, and then mix very well.

• Add seasonings to taste.

• Serve.

CAULIFLOWER MASH.

This is a smooth, healthy scrumptious delight that will make you feel good all through the evening. Aside from having simple ingredients, it can be prepared at a reasonably rapid rate too.

Cook Time: 10 mins

Prep Time: 5 mins

Serves: 8

Ingredients:

1 lb. cauliflower

6 oz. grated parmesan cheese

8 oz. butter

1 lemon, juice and zest

Ghee oil

Directions:

• Clean and chop cauliflower into florets.

• Put water into a medium-sized skillet, and then apply medium heat to it. Throw in the cauliflower and add a little salt to the mixture — it should be sufficient for the florets to become soft while retaining a fairly firm texture. Boil for about 2-3 minutes.

• Throw away the water.

• Get a food processor and throw in all the ingredients left together with the cauliflower and blend on high speed until your preferred consistency is attained.

• Add salt and pepper to taste.

• You may drizzle some olive oil over it if you want.

STUFFED MUSHROOM

The delicious stuffed mushroom is one of the healthiest sides you can find around, and is intended to give your ketosis a superb kick!

Cook Time: 20 mins

Prep Time: 10 mins

Serves: 4 (2 stuffed mushrooms)

Ingredients:

½ Tbsp. grass-fed ghee

1/8 Cup onion, chopped

3 cups fresh baby spinach

1/8 Tsp. freshly grated nutmeg

½ Tbsp. almond flour

⅓ Cup crumbled feta cheese

1/8 Tsp. Himalayan salt

1/8 Tsp. fresh black pepper, ground

8 big-sized mushrooms, cleaned, and stem cut off

Directions:

• Heat the oven up to 375 degrees Fahrenheit.

• Put ghee in a medium-sized skillet and apply medium-high heat to it until the oil heats up.

• Add the chopped onions and sauté for around 2 minutes until it becomes translucent.

• Throw in the spinach and cook for around 2 minutes till it becomes wilted.

• Put off the cooker, and introduce nutmeg, almond flour, and feta cheese into the mix. Arrange them on a baking sheet.

• Bake in the oven for around 15 minutes until mushrooms become tender.

SOUPS

A soup is a savory liquid dish made by combining fish, meat and veggies with stock or water along with other ingredients. Soups are usually served warm or hot.

A SOUP

EGG DROP SOUP

Cook Time: 20 mins

Prep Time: 10 mins

Serves: 2

Ingredients:

3 cups chicken broth

1 medium-sized carrot, peeled and cut into half moons

½ clove garlic, minced

⅛ Tsp. fresh ginger, grated

1 ½ Thai chilies, seeded and diced

1 ½ Tbsp. coconut aminos

2 large eggs, pastured

1 medium green onions, diced

1/8 cup fresh cilantro, chopped

Himalayan salt

Black pepper, freshly ground

Directions:

• Put chicken into a medium-sized saucepan with some water and apply high heat to it for around 10 minutes.

• As the chicken boils, throw in carrot, garlic, ginger, chilies, and coconut aminos. Reduce the heat and allow mixture to simmer for about 15 minutes and until the flavors develop and carrot becomes soft.

• Crack eggs into a small bowl and beat vigorously. Pour in the egg into the soup and stir mixture while pouring.

• Take away mixture from the cooker and throw in green onion and cilantro. Sprinkle salt and pepper over mixture to your taste.

BEEF AND CABBAGE SOUP

This hearty beef-based soup is inspired by cabbage and other healthy ingredients that will deliver a flavorful taste to your palate!

Cook Time: 20 mins

Prep Time: 10 mins

Serves: 4

Ingredients:

1 Tbsp. olive oil

1 large onion, chopped

1lb. Scotch fillet steak, cut into 1-inch pieces without visible fat

1 stalk celery chopped

1 large carrot, peeled and cubed

1 small green cabbage finely chopped

2 cloves garlic, minced

3 cups beef stock

1 ½ Tbsps. fresh chopped parsley and some more for serving

1 Tsp. dried thyme

1 Tsp. dried rosemary

1 Tsp. onion or garlic powder

Salt and freshly cracked black pepper to taste

Directions:

• Apply medium-heat to oil in a medium pot. Put in the beef and fry until it is brown on all sides while ensuring it doesn't burn.

• Add onions and cook for around 4 minutes, till it becomes transparent.

• Throw in the celery and carrots and let them blend in with the flavors in the pot by stirring a little. Cook mixture for around 3-4 minutes while stirring intermittently.

• Introduce cabbage into the mix and cook for another 5 minutes until it starts to become tender; put in the garlic, and then cook for about a minute until fragrant while stirring all the ingredients through.

• Add other ingredients like parsley, dried herbs, and onion or garlic powder along with the stock. Lower the heat, cover the pot with a lid and let it simmer.

• Let the mixture simmer for about 15 minutes, or when cabbage and carrots become tender.

• Put additional dried herbs, if you feel there is any need to. Sprinkle salt and pepper.

• Garnish with fresh parsley and serve soup while it is warm.

ZERO-NOODLE CHICKEN SOUP

This is the perfect meal that will enhance the immune system and help combat flu while delivering a dose of essential nutrients to your body system.

Cook Time: 20 mins

Prep Time: 10 mins

Serves: 4

Ingredients:

2 oz. butter

1½ celery stalks

3 oz. sliced mushrooms

1 garlic cloves, minced

1 Tbsp. dried minced onion

1 Tsp. dried parsley

1 Tsp. salt

1/8 Tsp. ground black pepper

4 cups chicken broth

1 medium-sized carrot

¾ shredded rotisserie chickens

1 cup green cabbage sliced into strips

Directions:

• Apply heat to a large pot with butter inside.

• Chop celery stalks and mushrooms into smaller pieces.

• Slice the celery stalks and mushrooms into smaller pieces.

• Throw in onion, celery, mushrooms and garlic into the pot and cook combination for about 4 minutes.

• Stir in the broth and add carrot, parsley, salt, and pepper. Allow it to simmer till veggies become soft.

• Put in the already cooked chicken and cabbage. Let the mixture boil for an extra 8-12 minutes till the cabbage "noodles" are soft.

SALADS

Aside from being an excellent option as a side dish, they also make great meals themselves — mostly for lunch. While there is a prevailing misconception that the conventional salads have a tendency of leaving one famished and unfulfilled, the same can't be said of keto salads because they are loaded with nutritious, flavorful veggies and fats to keep you going for the whole day.

SALAD

KALE AND AVOCADO SALAD

Cook Time: 20 mins

Prep Time: 10 mins

Yield: 2 servings

Ingredients:

For salad:

½ bunch of kale

½ Tbsp. olive oil

½ Tbsp. fresh lemon juice

1/8 Tsp. sea salt

For dressing:

1 avocado, chopped

½ Tbsp. olive oil

½ Tbsp. fresh lemon juice

½ Tsp. nutritional yeast

1/8 Tsp. sea salt

A pinch of black pepper

1 ½ Tbsp. pumpkin seeds for garnish

Directions:

• Separate hard stem from leaves of kale and arrange leaves on top of one other.

• Roll the leaves into a cigar-like tube and cut them into thin ribbons.

• Put kale ribbons inside a big bowl and drizzle olive oil over them. Also, add the lemon juice, and salt.

• Massage the kale for around 2 minutes, and watch it become greener in color. Put it aside.

For the dressing:

• In a food processor, add avocado, olive oil, lemon juice, nutritional yeast, salt and pepper, and then pulse until you get a smooth, creamy consistency.

• Toss massaged kale with dressing, and garnish with pumpkin seeds before serving!

KALE AND BLUEBERRY SALAD

This salad is just the right way to get loads of veggies into your keto meal while adding the sweet taste that blueberry brings without having to exceed your calorie intake!

Cook Time: 20 mins

Prep Time: 10 mins

Servings: 2

Ingredients:

3 oz. (170 g) kale, chopped roughly

5 blueberries

½ Tbsp. sliced almonds

1/8 red onion, cut into thin slices

½ Tbsp. parsley

½ Tbsp. lemon juice

1 Tbsp. olive oil

Salt and pepper to taste

Directions:

• Combine all the ingredients together.

• Share them between 2 plates and serve.

CHICKEN TONNATO

This salad packs plenty of nutritious ingredients in the form of chicken, spices, and leafy greens that will give your ketosis an immense boost.

Cook Time: 20 mins

Prep Time: 10 mins

Servings: 2

Ingredients:

Tonnato sauce

1 Tbsp. small capers

2 oz. tuna in olive oil

1 garlic cloves

1/8 cup fresh basil, chopped

½ Tsp. dried parsley

1 Tbsp. lemon juice

¼ cup mayonnaise

1/8 cup olive oil

¼ Tsp. salt

1/8 Tsp. ground black pepper

Chicken

12½ oz. chicken breasts

Water

Salt

3½ oz. leafy greens

Directions:

• With the exception of the tonnato sauce, put the rest of the ingredients for the sauce into a food processor and pulse them together. Keeping the tonnato will allow the flavors to evolve.

• Apply heat to a pot with slightly salted water, and put in the chicken breast to cook. When the water boils, get rid of the foam that emerges on the surface.

• Allow the mixture to boil for around 15 minutes on medium or till the chicken is completely cooked. Should you employ a meat thermometer, a reading of 165°F would indicate doneness.

• Let the mixture sit for no less than 10 minutes before cutting.

• Arrange leafy greens on serving plates and place the cut chicken on it.

• Dole out some spoonful of the sauce on the chicken.

• Serve with additional capers and a wedge of fresh lemon.

SEAFOOD AND AVOCADO SALAD

This salad presents you a unique opportunity to savor the delicious taste of shrimps and salmon, along with healthy fats intended to balance your ketogenic diet.

Cook Time: 20 mins

Prep Time: 0 mins

Servings: 3

Ingredients:

½ lb. cooked salmon, bite-sized pieces

½ lb. cooked shrimp, chopped

¼ cup avocados, chopped

1 Tbsp. lime juice

¼ cup mayonnaise

1/6 cup sour cream

1 garlic clove

½ Tsp. salt

1/8 Tsp. white pepper

¼ cup red onions, finely minced

1/6 cup cucumber, chopped

⅙ cup tomatoes, chopped

Directions:

• Put all the ingredients such as lime juice, mayonnaise, sour cream, garlic, salt, pepper, and minced onion into a mixing bowl and mix them properly.

• In another bowl, combine salmon, shrimp, avocado, cucumber, and tomato together. Afterward, put mayonnaise dressing over them, and toss gently to mix them properly.

• Allow the mixtures to cool for about 30 minutes before serving.

TUNA SALAD AND BOILED EGG

An easy-to-make salad that gives you the fantastic taste of tuna and boiled eggs all rolled into one — just to brighten your day.

Cook Time: 10 mins

Prep Time: 5 mins

Servings: 4

Ingredients:

8 oz. celery stalks

4 scallions

10 oz. tuna in olive oil

1 ½ cup mayonnaise

1 lemon, zest and juice

2 Tsp. Dijon mustard

8 pastured eggs

1 lb. Romaine lettuce

8 oz. cherry tomatoes

4 Tbsp. olive oil

salt and pepper

Directions:

• Prepare celery and scallions by chopping them finely. Put both of them in a medium-sized bowl and combine them with tuna, lemon, mayonnaise, and mustard.

• Stir to mix them properly, and then sprinkle some salt and pepper to taste. Set it aside for use later.

• Add water to a saucepan, then put the eggs and let them be entirely submerged by the water. Apply heat and let it boil for around 10 minutes.

• Remove the eggs and put them in ice-cold water straightaway when done. This is to make peeling them stress-free. Cut them up into halves.

• Arrange tuna mix and eggs on the already laid out romaine lettuce. Garnish with tomatoes and pour olive oil on top. Add salt and pepper to taste.

CHAPTER THIRTEEN: SMOOTHIES

They can be regarded as healthy milkshakes and represents an inventive way for keto dieters to meet up with their fat requirements — it is not unusual to find smoothies loaded with heavy cream, coconut oil, etc. In this chapter, you will find a few recipes that are healthy and keto-approved for your enjoyment.

DELICIOUS SMOOTHIES

ANTIOXIDANT SMOOTHIE

Not only does this smoothie pack a lot of nutrients such as healthy fats, and protein, it also gives you the vitality and refreshing taste of spinach. In fact, this smoothie will come in handy for your breakfast.

Prep Time: 10 mins

Serves: 4

Ingredients:

1 cup pumpkin seeds

2 cup of frozen mixed berries

1 cup unsweetened pomegranate juice

1 cup unsweetened almond milk

2 cup spinach

1 Tbsp. hulled hemp seeds

Directions:

• Put the pumpkin seeds in a food processor and pulse on high till they turn into powder.

• Add the rest of the ingredients to the food processor and blend on high-speed until you achieve a smooth consistency.

• Serve.

SPICED AVOCADO SMOOTHIE

This sugar-free smoothie harnesses the health benefits of ginger, turmeric, and creamy low-carb coconut milk. It is worthy to note that ginger and turmeric both have high antioxidants and anti-inflammatory properties — thus making this smoothie an ideal boost for your keto diet.

Prep Time: 15 mins

Serves: 4

Ingredients:

1 avocado

1 ½ cup full - fat coconut milk

½ cup almond milk

2 Tsp. ginger, freshly grated

1 Tsp. turmeric, freshly peeled and grated

2 Tsp. lemon

2 cup crushed ice

Stevia

Directions:

• Add almond milk, ginger, turmeric, lemon, avocado, and coconut milk to a food processor and pulse on low-speed until you achieve a smooth consistency.

• Add crushed ice and Stevia to the mixture and pulse on low-speed until it is smooth

• You may decide to alter the sweetness and tartness to your taste. Although, a dash of black pepper won't impact the taste of the smoothie considerably, but it will make the active ingredient in turmeric to be active and available.

SPICED AVOCADO SMOOTHIE

Drinking this detoxifying smoothie will provide you with the stimulating power of unsweetened cacao while you will find the subtle taste of coconut milk to be reinvigorating too.

Prep Time: 5 mins

Serves: 2

1 ½ cup of coconut milk

1 ripe avocado

4 Tsp. unsweetened cacao powder

2 Tsp. cinnamon powder

½ Tsp. vanilla extract

Stevia to taste

1 Tsp. coconut oil

Directions:

- Put all the ingredients into a food mixer and blend them together

- Serve.

GREEN SMOOTHIE

This smoothie has the perfect combination of ingredients that will energize you throughout the day.

Prep Time: 5 mins

Yield: 5 ounces

Ingredients:

4 oz. almond milk

½ measure Perfect Keto Micronutrients Greens Powder in Orange

½ Tbsp. Perfect Keto C8 MCT oil

½ Tsp. orange zest

½ Tbsp. lemon juice

½ Tbsp. lime juice

½ handful ice

1/16 teaspoon xanthum gum

½ handful of spinach

Directions:

• Put all the ingredients in a food processor and pulse on high speed until you get a smooth consistency.

GREEN TEA DETOX SMOOTHIE

If there is a drink that can refresh and reinvigorate you in the morning, then this smoothie is what you need and will really help you get up to speed.

Prep Time: 5 mins

Serves: 4

Ingredients:

4 ounces of water

4 Tsp. Match Green Tea powder

2 cup sliced cucumber

4 ounces ripe avocado

2 Tsp. lemon juice

1 Tsp. lemon liquid stevia

1 cup ice

Directions:

• Put water and green tea powder into a food processor and pulse it on high speed to mix.

• Put in the rest of the ingredients and pulse on high until it reaches a smooth consistency.

• Adjust the quantity of sweetener you desire by tasting it.

• Put in the fridge or serve right away.

FROZEN BERRY SHAKE

This is a tasty delight with mixed berries as its base, and is designed strictly for your enjoyment!

Prep Time: 5 mins

Serves: 2

Ingredients:

1/6 cup creamed coconut milk

1 cup almond milk

1 cup mixed berries, frozen

2 Tbsp. coconut oil

1 cup ice or more

Optionally add:

10 Drops Stevia extract

1 Tsp. sugar-free vanilla extract

Whipped cream as topping

Directions:

• Put ingredients like creamed coconut milk, berries, and almond milk into a food processor and blend them properly on high speed.

• Introduce MCT oil and stevia to the mix.

• Blend until you get a smooth consistency and serve instantly.

• Use whipped cream as the topping.

CONCLUSION

In conclusion, this book has successfully gone through the fundamentals of the ketogenic diet and will serve as a valuable guide for beginners intending to go on this diet because it has essential tips and guides that they will find helpful in their quest to live a healthy life. Furthermore, there are keto-approved meal recipes that they can fall back on should they have to fit this unique lifestyle into a busy schedule. From breakfasts, snacks, and dinners, to sides, mains, salads, soups, and smoothies — the quick and easy-to-make recipes in this book are designed to mentor them all the way to achieving their health and fitness goals.

Made in the USA
Columbia, SC
28 March 2019